The Lost Art of Planning Projects

The Lost Art of Planning Projects

Louise Worsley and Christopher Worsley

BEP BUSINESS EXPERT PRESS

The Lost Art of Planning Projects

First published in 2019 by
Business Expert Press, LLC
222 East 46th Street, New York, NY 10017
www.businessexpertpress.com

ISBN-13: 978-1-94858-069-4 (paperback)
ISBN-13: 978-1-94858-070-0 (e-book)

Business Expert Press Portfolio and Project Management Collection

Collection ISSN: 2156-8189 (print)
Collection ISSN: 2156-8200 (electronic)

Cover and interior design by Exeter Premedia Services Private Ltd., Chennai, India

First edition: 2019

10 9 8 7 6 5 4 3 2 1

Printed in the United States of America.

Abstract

Appropriate planning is the hallmark of professional project management. Good planning is what sets apart great projects from accidents. Purposeful planning is what ensures that the executive actions undertaken remain connected to the goals and outcomes expected by the stakeholders.

This book examines the process and products of planning, in the contexts of projects, programs, and portfolios. With a plan seen as a model, it looks at how the use of models in planning creates and extends the way in which project, program, and portfolio managers control and structure their environment.

To tell this story, we have distilled over 70 years of our combined personal experience of supporting project managers deliver, and thousands of person-years of others' practical knowledge to illustrate powerful planning tools, models, and approaches. There is also supplementary material and tools on a website associated with this book. We hope you find this useful as you plan your next great project!

Keywords

Agile; portfolio management; program management; project constraints; project management; project planning; scope management

Contents

Preface

Research on high performing project managers found that of the top five activities they attended to, planning always featured. So, we were disappointed when a recent review of project governance practices in five large project organizations reported that evidence of planning taking place in projects was sometimes difficult to find.

While outputs from the concept, initiation, and closure stages were consistently present and easily trackable, outputs from planning were not. What a planning document consisted of also varied widely between projects, project managers, and stages within the project. In over a quarter of the projects in the planning stage or beyond, it was not possible to locate any recognizable project plan! The follow-up discussions with project managers revealed surprisingly diverse and inventive explanations as to why planning documents were 'unavailable.'

Perhaps the 'no-plan' projects can be forgiven when you discover that some—perhaps many—business and IT project managers have never experienced, or been taught, the process of project planning. For them, planning is either creating a to-do list, setting out a schedule, or, in the worst case, completing a template supplied by their project management office. In the latter case, the resulting plans are a perfect example of 'make-work': done for compliance reasons and never referenced again during the life of the project.

This lack of planning discipline is important for two reasons. Firstly: despite the much-reported fact that successful delivery by projects is 'patchy,' with the Standish Report (2016) commenting that under 40 percent deliver what was anticipated, organizations still find them to be the best management vehicles for causing planned change to happen. Secondly, what projects are now expected to deliver has evolved, with outputs and outcomes much more complicated and more complex than was the case from the 1950s to the late 1980s.

The surge in the number of projects and their rising complexity has seen some response by the project management profession, but planning has largely been neglected. Indeed, in some quarters the need for it has even been challenged.

The introduction of Agile, a software product development framework, is having a significant and positive impact upon the way IT projects are delivered. However, we also find confusion among project managers. Some experienced project managers quickly learn how to adapt and integrate Agile practices into their toolset. It is just another approach, which used appropriately on the right projects, increases their ability to deliver. Others move straight to denial; change-weary, they avoid or downplay the usefulness of the Agile framework—"It's nothing new." That is their loss! Of greater concern are the more junior project managers who, faced with Agilists, lose their bearings. "What is my role in this?" "How does governance work?" "How do I plan?" And most worrying—"Do I need a plan?"

This book is for all those who know the answer to that question is most definitely "Yes," and would like to know more. Portfolio managers, program managers, and PMO managers need to understand how and when to plan. So do project managers. The planning approaches they adopt differ as will the content because the context and purpose of the plans differ. We look at what a plan is for—what its functions are. We discuss what should be in a plan, and what factors influence the contents.

There are no templates because templates kill planning. There are, however, many models, tools, techniques, tips, and tricks to support the process of planning, and provide ways of making planning a purposeful and powerful contributor to the success of portfolios, programs, and projects.

These are the questions we have tried to answer:

1. What makes a good plan, and how can you recognize one?
2. How can you *ensure* that work done, effort expended, and outputs produced deliver the stakeholders agenda? How do you manage the bridge between vision and action?
3. How do you develop a plan that satisfies the five functions every project plan has?
4. How can you establish and maintain the optimum strategic project portfolio?
5. In what ways are the planning processes for portfolios, programs, and projects different?
6. What factors and experiences will help you become a better planner?

Acknowledgments

This book is the result of the input and support from many colleagues and fellow project managers. Particular thanks are due to the patient reviewers who endured and provided feedback on our early endeavors: Jane Nichols, Hilary Small, Tania Heydenrych, Johnathan Norman, Juliet Doswell, Jeandré Williams, and Ken Burrell. And without Professor Tim Kloppenborg's encouragement, we would never have done it. Thank you to them all.

Many of the models and techniques discussed in this book were developed, taught, and deployed by CITI. CITI is a UK project management company that has specialized in developing personal and organizational capability in the running of projects and programs in large corporations and government since 1991. This book serves as a repository of the knowledge, skills, and commitment of all the members of CITI, and a record of clients CITI has been privileged to support to make their projects and programs a success.

Writing this book caused us to revisit more than 25 years of working with organizations and individuals to develop and deliver projects and programs—either directly—or like midwives, helping to bring new capabilities and new ambitions to life. The people we have worked with, whether members of CITI, our project management company in the UK or PiCubed, its sister company in South Africa, or the hundreds of amazing clients, each of whom made a contribution to our understanding, and through that to the contents of this book, thank you.

CHAPTER 1

The Principles of Planning

Planning as Modeling

It's worth saying right from the start that a plan is merely a model of the real world. Once you have a plan, as soon as the real world diverges from it you know something you didn't know before. With a plan, every divergence gives you the opportunity to revise your approach, change your assumptions, and learn. Without a plan, you are a passive follower, being led by the circumstances that arise. This is why planning is so important, and why it is necessarily iterative.

So what makes a good model? Every good model is an abstraction of reality—a simplification. It must represent correctly and usefully those aspects of reality that interest you. It can, and often does, ignore less relevant bits. Good models don't attempt to capture everything—just what's relevant. The project manager needs simplicity: simplification without being simplistic. This leads us to the first summary point:

SP1: Plans focus on what is contextually important

In fact, it is common for models to distort reality. Take the way the world is modeled in maps. The Earth is an oblate sphere, an awkward shape to carry around. What we want is a two-dimensional model that allows us to navigate, to assess land acreage, or perhaps to establish international boundaries. The problem is that you cannot do all of these on any one map with the same degree of accuracy and confidence.

Just look at Australia or Greenland in the three maps shown in Figure 1.1. Which is the real shape? Well, none of them! The better question is: What do I want to do, and which projection makes that easiest for me?

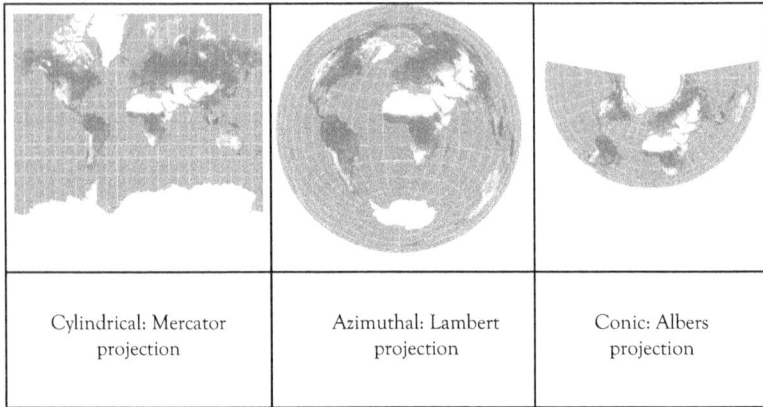

| Cylindrical: Mercator projection | Azimuthal: Lambert projection | Conic: Albers projection |

Figure 1.1 Different projections of Earth

Cylindrical, conic, and azimuthal are the commonest projections used to represent the Earth on a flat sheet of paper. Each has a method for translating spatial dimensions. Each has its advantages, and each creates problems.

And so it is with models for project planning. There are different approaches that when used in the appropriate circumstances provide better insights and make the planning more directly useful. No single approach is the right approach, which leads to:

SP2: Different types of project initiatives require different types of plan

That portfolios, programs, and different types of projects require different types of plans is the thesis of this book. It affects every aspect, including what is planned, how it is planned, and when it is planned.

Different models examine different aspects of reality; so many different models exist. Searching for a single unifying theory linking them together may be a doomed exercise, and it is not necessary. The correct description of the project or the world is never more than a snapshot capturing the current 'moment of truth.' As perspectives change, and with it our understanding, what counts as truth also changes. Planning is the same. A plan is a view of a future state the project is purposed to achieve. As things change, in particular as stakeholder perceptions of what 'good looks like' changes, the plan must reflect this, so:

SP3: Plans evolve, reflecting the changing multiple perspectives of the stakeholders

Finally, the greater the number of analogs and the larger the number of inferences suggested by the model, the more valuable it is. This is the power of a model; it helps to uncover and discover factors that otherwise might have been overlooked as you move from the known to the less certain. A good model lets you make predictions about a future state that you would not be able to make from inspecting the current situation: precisely what a plan needs to do. It turns out that:

SP4: The process of planning is at least as important as the products of planning

Five Functions of a Project Plan

This book is not about planning; it is about planning projects. So, we had better set out what we mean by 'projects.' We base our definition on formulations given over the years by Turner (1999, 2003).

A *project* is a temporary organization set up to manage the inherent uncertainty caused when resources are assigned to undertake a unique and transient endeavor within a set of constraints and needs to integrate the outputs created into a changed future state that delivers beneficial outcomes.

The definition is rather long, but it does capture all the essential elements.

- Projects are temporary structures, and they have to be granted authority from their parent organization to deliver specific objectives—they are goal-driven endeavors.
- Projects are unique, or at least 'relatively unique' (perhaps done before, but not by this team, or in this way), projects must actively manage uncertainty.
- Project success is largely determined by stakeholders believing that the project was a direct contributor to a sustained changed state that they regard as good, or at least an improvement.

- Finally, the role of constraints is highlighted in Turner's (2003) definition. Their significance in the planning and execution of a project is the subject of much of this chapter, and the rest of the book.

Every project is a collaboration to bring about an agreed future state, and to achieve that there needs to be a plan and that plan needs to fulfill four functions. Let us look briefly at them.

Plan as a Snapshot

A plan translates today into tomorrow

Project planning is part of the way we manage uncertainty. A plan is a view of the future, created from the state of knowledge at that time, and supported and extended by the inferences that experience and the under-pinning models provide. As knowledge increases that view may change, and the new route to the future must be captured in the plan.

Let us suppose that the way to procure a service for your project is unclear. In the plan, you allocate two specialist resources for two months of elapsed time to deliver it. After a week, these experts advise you that the service is in great demand so there will be delays lasting well beyond the two months set aside. The plan is invalid! You need to re-plan. You advise the stakeholders; you re-organize the team; there are no surprises. The project may be delayed, and if time is of the essence, even canceled, but nothing has gone wrong. Uncertainty about acquiring the service has been reduced by buying information (in this case, recruiting experts to resolve the procurement concern), and the new knowledge resulted in re-planning. Can it get better than that?

A plan that documents exactly what everyone already knows really is a waste of everyone's time, no matter how beautifully written. It is the worst form of bureaucracy, with nothing new learned and nothing valuable achieved. A good plan makes clear what is uncertain and why, and what to do about it. What is known and what is not should be reflected in the very structure of the plan. What is certain is why the project was set up. We also know what the stakeholders' regard as a good outcome. What is less certain is what the right tactics to adopt might be. These are uncertain because currently unknown events, events in the future, will influence them; whether it is by time passing, from the impact of risks, or higher than expected levels of productivity of a process.

The mixture of known and unknown, of the certain, the expected but unknown, and the unknown unknowns form the material for the plan. Their specific combination makes the plan a snapshot of the project at a moment in time.

And, of course, as the future happens, some things that were uncertain become certain, and new options become available, new future states. This is the basis for plans evolving, and why plans must be snapshots, reflecting the changing understanding of the project audiences. It is also why considering plans to be a set of rails that takes you from the start to the end and upon which the project train has to run else it will fail, is a mistake. Plans are *not* the best document for telling you what to do, and when to do it. You need a schedule to do that.

Plan as a Map

A plan is more than a schedule

A good project plan describes how to achieve the project goal in the context of the 'territory.' It shows how the parent organization, the local project environment, and any competing projects affect it. The plan helps to determine where you are and how to get to your goal, even when you have been driven off course. In many ways, a project plan acts much like a map. A map is also a model of the world. While plans have assumptions, constraints, risks, and so on; maps make use of rivers, roads, towns, and so on, as their constituent parts.

Let's use the road map shown in Figure 1.2. It is a bit of Italy, with Rome set in the center.

Rome is, of course, our objective—after all, all roads lead to Rome! We started at Artema. To the left of us is the Mediterranean—that's a definite risk—the car can't swim. To the right are the Appalachian Mountains. They are a threat too—another risk—as the car doesn't do well in mountainous country—it consumes vast amounts of fuel. Among the many constraints, one is that we really must stay on the main roads. In Italy, some minor roads shown on the map don't actually exist, and there are only two days to make this journey.

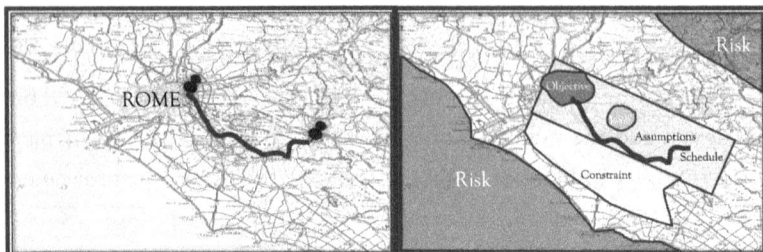

Figure 1.2 Plan as a map

There is also an issue. It is in the town called Frascati. I have relatives there. Do we have to go via that town? A 'yes' decision could make achieving the objective of 'arriving in Rome in a happy state of mind' a little harder, as they can really be very demanding!

And, as you can see, the route has been identified. It sets out where we will be and when, just like a project schedule.

My partner is driving; I'm navigating. At some point, and for reasons too obscure to discuss here, we end up in a little place called Aprilia. Clearly, off route—what is to be done? Do we go back? That would inevitably entail doing activities and spending petrol and time not included in the original schedule (no one had discussed backtracking) or do we re-plan and establish another route?

To backtrack or to re-plan are two critical project questions. A project manager should always be able to answer them. Without a plan, there is no rational basis to make the decision. A plan makes it possible to have an informed debate.

This example also makes clear the difference between having a plan—a map—and a schedule—a route. If all you have is a route, success is sticking to it. Once off the route, you are lost! Project management is *not* progress-chasing; a mechanism designed to keep the project on the schedule. It is about control, and about responding to changing circumstances and achieving the project goals despite becoming temporarily uncertain of your position.

Plan as a Communication

Purposeful communication goes beyond transmitting ideas-it is more about influence

Whatever else a plan is and does, it is always a communication vehicle. It conveys information, sets expectations, and allows decisions to be made. How well plans do communicate can be a little haphazard, and that needs to be fixed.

Effective communication occurs when the specific needs of the audience are addressed. Different audiences have different needs, that's why they are different! Using templated documents is unlikely to meet this condition. (When assessing high performing project managers, we find that they consistently adapt their plans, reports, summaries, and presentations to suit their audience. They focus on what the audience needs to know and find memorable ways of getting that information across.)

A project plan is unique among the set of governance documents used to run a project in that it has *two* audiences. This does make the writing of it a little harder. One audience is the governance group—and sometimes more widely the key stakeholders—the other is the project team. However, the communication purpose is singular, and that is to provide these audiences with enough 'big picture' context and information so that they know how they can best be involved in supporting and achieving the project's objective.

Informing them is different from telling them what they are to do or even expected to do. There are other project documents for doing that. One such is the schedule. A schedule is a detailed—possibly hour-by-hour specification of what each team member should do. A plan, on the other hand, is successful when the readers can identify how they will be impacted by what it is proposing to achieve, and how they can affect it—what and how they can contribute to further its achievement.

The following story rather nicely demonstrates this point. Toilet hygiene is important—even in prisons—and in prisons, inmates do the cleaning. In one prison, the plan for getting a clean toilet looked like this:

- Clean pan with a supplied brush
- Wipe rim with cleaning tissue
- Mop round base of the bowl
- Replace paper if reel empty
- Wipe seat with cleaning tissue
- Flush toilet

This is an example of procedural planning. It uses a combination of orders, regulations, methods, and procedures, and demands compliance. Such a plan, to be well written and useful, must specify the sequence of activities; the situation involved must be 'ordinary'; the tasks must be easily and reliably identifiable; and the 'how to' well defined and in line with known, well-understood current practices.

In another prison, the plan was different. It read like this:

- Inside pan to be visibly clean
- Toilet roll sufficient for 24 hours use
- Seat to be visibly and hygienically clean
- Toilet flushing mechanism to operate correctly
- Surrounding area to be visibly and hygienically clean

This is positive planning. It relies on defining 'what good looks like'; requires active decision making by subordinates; with direction and monitoring carried out by 'leaders.' It is based on defining outcomes, not inputs. Such plans recognize that choices of action are possible and viable, the situation can be dynamic, task identification can be difficult for subordinates, and task achievement often involves multiple interactions.

Who won? Which had the cleaner toilets? It may be obvious to you, but it came as a distinct shock to one of the prison wardens. Positive planning, planning that allowed the participants to contribute, gave rise to much, much cleaner, more hygienic toilets.

One of the principles of good planning is to allow subordinates and contributors the maximum degree of decision and action, with control only exercised to the extent necessary to provide the guidance and resources needed to accomplish tasks. Over-planning, as typified by procedural planning, can lead to an overemphasis on the process, and insufficient focus on the outcome—on efficiency rather than effectiveness.

There is a place for procedural planning—sometimes. We will discuss when it is appropriate later, but for now let us ask, "Does the plan get across what needs to be achieved, and does it convey how achievement

Empowering your team members to have authority over their portion of the project is invaluable.

There's little opportunity for micro-management in a constantly changing environment.

will be measured (monitored)?" In other words, is the plan understandable to everyone who needs to use it?

Plan as an Engagement

Plans are worthless; planning is everything

Many leaders and generals have commented on plans and their relative utility when it comes to war, but everyone agrees that planning is essential. Without planning there is no forum to gain agreement, there is no clarity about the outcomes; without planning, sources of uncertainty cannot be articulated into estimates; without planning there is no vehicle to compare and contrast solutions regarding desirability and degree of risk. But, and most importantly of all, without planning the best opportunity to engage, and to engage with stakeholders, is lost.

Because of all these reasons, and most especially the last, planning is not something project managers do on their own. Yes, they need input from sponsors and requirements-givers, and yes, they may need specialist knowledge from subject matter experts on the solutions and processes, and yes, they may need help drafting the words, but the real purpose of collaborating is none of these. What a perceptive project manager will recognize is that this engagement is not simply an information-gathering exercise. Actually, it is the very best mechanism by which the project builds support for the outcomes, and creates the energy and commitment to the delivery of the solution. It's the very basis upon which useful contribution to the project is founded.

The Agile approach, which encourages collaborative structures during the product development stage, absolutely understands this. They recognize the need to build the energy and start collaborative connections between team players that are so critical to the anticipation and joint resolution of problems further down the line.

In Chapter 6, we discuss project managers' skills and competencies and show that an appreciation of planning is fundamental to maturing project capability. Our research found that high performing project managers were much better at structuring the involvement of appropriate stakeholders in the planning process. It is not just about *doing* planning but about *facilitating* a discussion.

Plan as an Agreement

We have a tentative agreement; I expect no changes!

If a plan is a description of an uncertain future state and is subject to evolutionary change, how can it also be an agreement? What exactly is being agreed to? In the construction and engineering industries, plans often become an integral part of the contract. This can lead to problems. To avoid project objectives being taken as legal obligations, many contracts are a minefield of variance clauses and special conditions. The plan as a snapshot, as a map of the territory, and as a vehicle for communication has been sacrificed to the needs of legal enforcement of an agreement.

Many project managers, and perhaps especially IT project managers, may recognize the dangers of making an agreement about what the project will deliver too early. They know that setting expectations very early in the development life cycle is best avoided. Certainly making commitments too soon is a fraught process, but when is 'too soon?' Sponsors want commitment early. The doers prefer a later time. Boehm (1981) captured this dilemma well in his description of the 'cone of uncertainty.' Figure 1.3 (An Agile adapted version of the cone) urges the developer to be 'honest.' Sponsors, however, tend to view this honesty as prevarication, naiveté, lack of commitment, or all three.

Planning, as essential in Agile projects as in every other type of project, is about the need to 'contain' uncertainty and set out an agreement between the sponsor and the doer.

So, although to a developer not making promises in the darker grey area in Figure 1.3 makes sense, there are some caveats that need to be considered. Firstly, the sources and levels of uncertainty vary and waiting

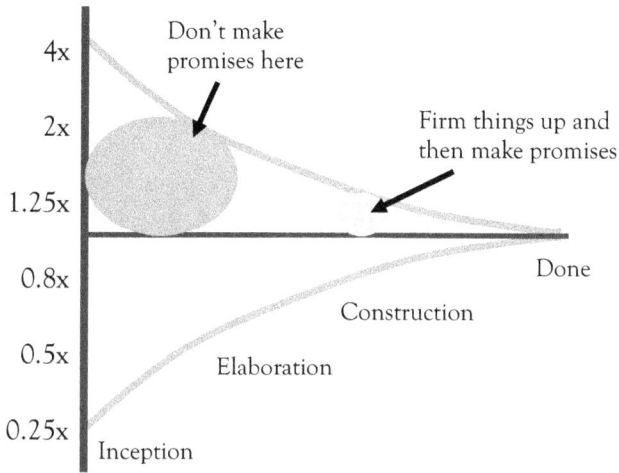

Figure 1.3 When to commit

Adapted from McConnell (2006).

is not the only reduction strategy. Secondly, and as we shall see through-out the book, establishing the constraints, be it end-date, fixed price or some other hard boundary condition, sets precisely what the project *has to* deliver.

Projects are uncertain endeavors, and the project plan sets expectations by describing a possible and acceptable route to delivery. So is it an agree-ment? A plan sets the baseline expectations while capturing the uncer-tainty and risks that must be addressed as the project progresses. A *good* plan will give sufficient confidence to stakeholders that they feel able to make decisions and engage resources. That is why it is an agreement.

When to Plan

The project plan is the third of three initial management deliverables that support the governance of a project. It should come after the motivation document and the business case, and definitely be finalized before the end of the project.

We have found, when we audit projects, a growing tendency to con-flate and even confuse the different documents. Sometimes the writers, having recognized that the governance documents inherit information and detail from their predecessors, see an opportunity to reduce effort. There is some merit in that. One of the most egregious errors found, when conducting project assurance reviews, is for content already agreed in previous governance documents to be rewritten without any attempt at re-authorization.

Nevertheless, trying to be 'economical' by using a compound document serving as a motivation document, business case, and plan all rolled into one is a grave mistake. These are three documents; each has a different purpose, different audiences, different life histories, and different accountabilities.

The motivation document comes first. It should identify the problem or opportunity, explaining why addressing it is valuable to the organization, and who thinks so. It is, in essence, the value proposition for the project.

The second document is the business case. Its role is to help choose the right project. It should *inherit* the problem/opportunity statement, the stakeholders' attitudes, and the benefits (either benefits or wanted impacts) from the motivation document. If there are any changes, which there could well be, they are introduced, with a note identifying the source and authority for the alterations. The new material in the business case relates to the constraints, the critical success factors (CSFs), the options considered as possible solutions, costs, and any risks to the achievement of the benefits and the conduct of the project.

Then there is the project plan; its function is to identify how to run the project in the right way. This sequence does *not* imply that the plan must come—and can only come—before the project starts. Traditionally this was so, but a review of the four perspectives discussed earlier makes clear this was never true. Planning is an activity that takes place when the project needs to manage uncertainty, and that can occur throughout its life.

The Parts of a Plan

Any model—and hence any plan—can be reduced to three components. The architectonic—the structure, or if you like, the rooms and 'spaces' any plan has. The constitutive elements—the 'furniture' that can be found in those spaces. And the third component, the regulative principles—the rules that relate one constitutive element to the others.

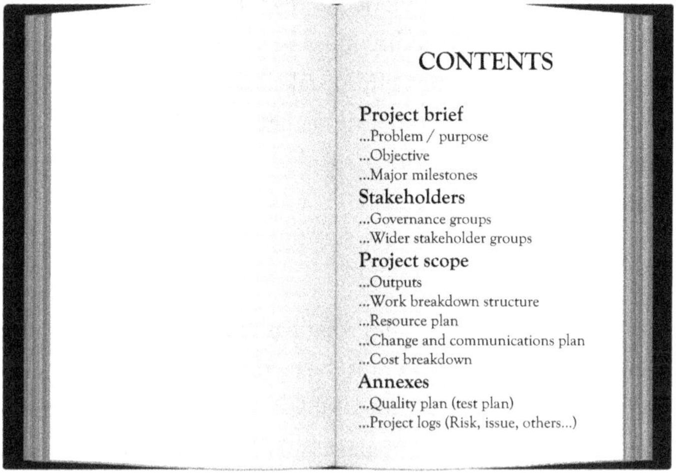

CONTENTS

Project brief
...Problem / purpose
...Objective
...Major milestones
Stakeholders
...Governance groups
...Wider stakeholder groups
Project scope
...Outputs
...Work breakdown structure
...Resource plan
...Change and communications plan
...Cost breakdown
Annexes
...Quality plan (test plan)
...Project logs (Risk, issue, others...)

Figure 1.4 Contents of a typical project plan

In a project plan, the architectonic is physically set out in the contents pages of the governance documents. Different plans have different contents, but those listed in Figure 1.4 are essential and should always feature somewhere.

The text of the project brief and the information about the stakeholders are inherited, either verbatim or as amended by authorized changes, from the motivation and business case documents. One of the more challenging aspects of project management is gaining commitment from stakeholders, so the process of maintaining their voice in the project plan is so important. Paying attention to this by *not* rewriting their agreed text goes some way to achieving this.

The plan should also be structured to make it easy to monitor and to maintain. This suggests organizing the document to reflect the different volatilities of its constituent components. A project plan thus tends to fall naturally into four parts.

Part A: The Strategic Component

The first part, Part A, describes the strategic intent of the project. It is made up of the sections called the 'Project brief,' and 'Stakeholders.' Some think of this as the project charter. Whatever its name, its content, format, and style should be concise, motivating, and in compelling prose. Its source, authority, and validity must be visible, with clear traceability of its evolution and agreement from stakeholders. The first few pages of the plan are generally subject to little change, though changes in the environment, technology, and more particularly the stakeholders, can and do cause evolution of the text.

Part B: The Tactical Component

The second part, Part B, identifies what has to be done and how it will be done—the scope of the project. It is the tactical part of the plan and rarely benefits from being in flowing text. Table 1.1 shows an example extract of a tabulated format. All project managers we know seem to love Excel! The columns capture four of the constitutive elements of the plan: the outputs with estimates of size and number, the processes, the resources, and any risks associated with the outputs, the processes, and the resources.

At this point in the planning, all that needs to be known is whether the chosen process is standard, whether the source of the resource is known, and what the apparent risks are. (The detail of the non-standard processes, and the description and management of the risks are set out in the appropriate logs when the information becomes available.)

The status of the project—how near to completion it is—is monitored easily by plotting the delivery of outputs. (Figure 1.5 is an example of a product count or delivery status graph).

Table 1.1 A tabulated plan

| Product | Number required | | Process | Resources | Risks |
	Low	High			
Software licenses	2,400	2,400	Std	Procurement	None: fixed price
Hardware upgrades	400	550	Std	IT	Number of upgrades needed uncertain
Dept, servers	5	7	Std	IT	No agreement from Depts. on server upgrades
Trained-operators	5	7	Std	Ops	Unsure of the amount of training time
Trained staff	2,000	2,400	New	HRD	No agreement on training approach or how long it will take

Product completion

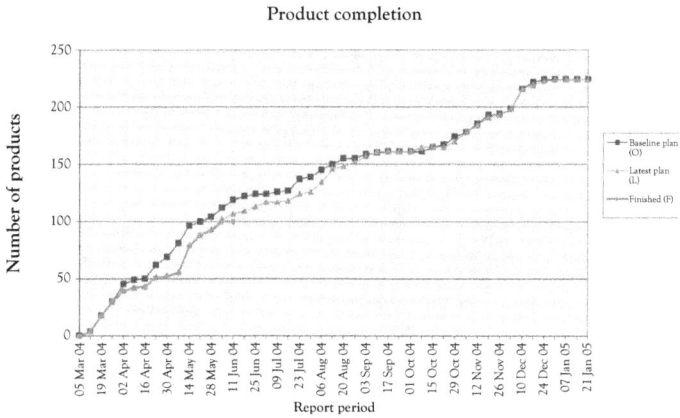

Figure 1.5 A delivery status chart

Part B of a plan is subject to considerably more change than Part A. As the predicted dates for completion vary from the original, the delivery status chart is updated. Changes to the resources, products, and processes must also be captured. As these latter two modify the scope of the project, the changes should be subject to some form of configuration control management system. This part and the next part, Part C, are what many people mean when they talk of a project's management plan or PMP.

Part C: The Logs

Part C contains the other nine constitutive elements of a plan. Table 1.2 lists them. Information on their status is held in a log that is set up for each of them.

Table 1.2 The nine project logs

Stakeholders log
Assumptions log
Constraints log
Log of changes
Risk log
Issue log
Dependencies log
Decisions log
Log of agreed actions

Each log should be subject to continuing change as entries are made and updated. Indeed one of the first ports of call when conducting a project assurance process is to check the logs. Projects whose logs remain unchanged for days at a time are likely to be undermanaged. We will discuss logs, how they are used in planning and management, in more detail in Chapter 3. Monitoring of Part C is best carried out by maintaining 'aging' reports for each of the logs, showing the rate at which new entries come on, the age of entries that remain 'active,' and the rate of closure.

Part D: The Schedule

The final section of the plan, Part D, is the most volatile component. It is the schedule.

The regulative principles link the various constitutive elements together, organizing them to achieve the project's objective. In a project plan, the rules are about: how work can be allocated across resources; how information is transferred; what counts as 'being complete'; who has authority to decide what; and how effort time can be packed into calendar time.

Application of these rules appropriately creates a schedule, a mechanism for structuring work that gets you from where you are to where you want to be. Within it, the most stable components should be the major milestones, but even they can be subject to significant variation. Monitoring schedules can be an arduous and time-consuming task. One visual and straightforward technique is to use an adaptation of a slip chart shown in Figure 1.6. Easy to produce, it does convey the underlying dynamic of the

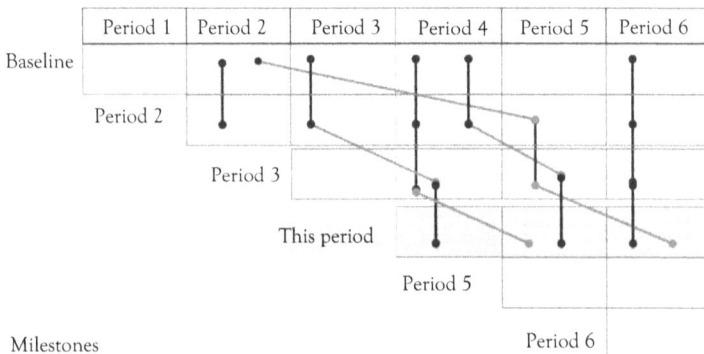

Figure 1.6 A modified slip chart

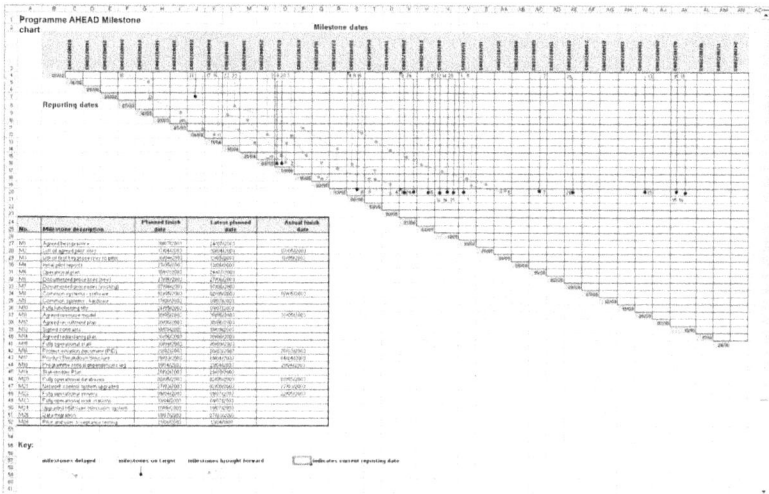

Figure 1.7 What a real one looks like

project. Figure 1.7 is what a real one looks like and shows the monitoring of a program selling off building assets. You can see there is a strong drift to the right, indicating severe slip. It also shows the characteristic belief that project managers have that future milestones will be kept to schedule (those nice straight lines on the right), until, of course, they get closer!

Purposeful Planning

To plan successfully, you must know what counts as a success, and over the years, this has changed. Once upon a time, it was said that a project had to meet three conditions: being on time, being within budget, and delivering the outputs. Now that is not enough. Shenhar et al. (1997) sum up the current view. There are, they say, four dimensions to satisfy:

- project efficiency
- impact on the customer
- direct business and organizational success
- preparing for the future

The first factor neatly bundles up the earlier ideas about traditional project management disciplines. The second and third reflect the growing realization that unless the project returns something of recognized value, its performance in terms of delivering the outputs requested is worthless. The fourth focuses on what it is that the stakeholders have to bring to the party. It is their role to identify and develop the future capability of the organization, to invest in organizational assets.

This modern view of projects recognizes that success is not solely determined by the management actions of the project manager, but by how history passes judgment on the value of the project—an uncomfortable situation for some project managers.

Figure 1.8 illustrates how the project success factors change with time. What is happening is that the mix of stakeholders who are making the judgments is changing. The influence and interest of the role-based stakeholders—stakeholders who are involved in the local governance of the project—wanes. The agenda-based stakeholders—stakeholders who have an emotional or specific agenda associated with the project— become more significant. (For more information on types of stakeholders, see Worsley 2016.)

Shenhar et al. (1997) in describing success dimensions over time suggest that projects must be planned to take into account not only the near-term success factors but also the long-term goals. Given that project success is ultimately judged by all the projects' stakeholders, this

1 Project efficiency
2 Impact on the end user
3 Direct business and organizational success
  Preparing for the future

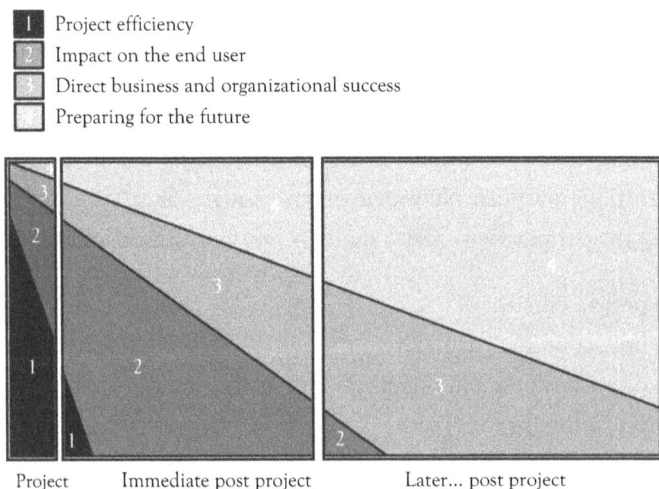

Project   Immediate post project   Later... post project

Figure 1.8 Effect of the passage of time on project success factors

Source: Shenhar et al. (1997).

necessitates consideration, not just of stakeholders close to the project, but also those individuals and groups who will be impacted in the near and longer terms.

So how do you go about developing a project plan that delivers success when time, cost, and quality constraints are not the focus? Is there a set process?

The answers are: there is a process; it varies, and the determining factors are the project's CSFs and the 'hierarchy of constraints.' The planning process, the sequence of steps, and the models differ, and the choice is based, not on the content of the project, but on the conditions of success.

The Role of Constraints and Critical Success Factors

When discussing project performance with CEOs of large corporations, we ask them to list the projects that they thought had met their criteria of being successful and well run. The similarities in their responses are striking. Projects mandated by legislation always featured, and sometimes they were the only ones on the list. Why was this, we wondered? What made them special? Well, the CEOs said, the objective was crystal clear, the end-dates were immovable, and getting the necessary resources uncontested. "Why then," we ask, "do they think other projects fail?" And their response: "I've no idea!"

Conversations like this led us to develop the Project Mission Model™, and the planning model discussed in Chapter 2. The coordination of six distinct elements: problem, objective, CSFs, products (outputs), benefits (value), and risks, together with the assumptions and constraints completely define the project. And, of all of these factors, it was the CSFs and the constraints that shaped the planning. So, what are they, and how do they act in this way?

Constraints

Let us start by looking at constraints.

Constraints feature in Turner's definition of a project quoted earlier, and in the PMI's definition, published in 2017:

A project is a planned set of interrelated tasks to be executed over a fixed period and within certain cost and other limitations. (PMI 2017)

Goldratt and Cox (1984) in their excellent book *The Goal* popularized the concept of constraints and the Theory of Constraints. They define constraints as elements that impede progress toward achieving the goal. While true for operational management perhaps, this is a somewhat misleading definition for project managers. It might even be the cause of such statements as, *The limitations imposed by my budget / deadline / the resources were the cause of my project's failure.* Worse still if it leads to project managers, in their struggle to succeed, to actively subvert, or disregard their project's constraints!

A much more helpful view for a project manager is that derived from mathematics where a constraint is, *...a condition ...that the solution must satisfy.* With this perspective, it becomes clear that the role of a project constraint is to help define what a successful solution looks like—it is a condition that a possible successful approach must fulfill. It should also be clear why constraints can *never* be project risks, can *never* be project issues, as they are in fact a prerequisite for project success.

A *constraint* is a boundary value which if breached means that the project plan is invalid and the project is working beyond its remit.

A constraint is 'owned' by someone other than the project manager.

The 2017 PMI definition of a project has not moved far from the traditional view that a project is a time-bounded activity: a set of delivered capabilities, within a budget, by an end-date. It suggests that not meeting these three conditions means project failure.

A moment's reflection shows this is facile; it is patently false for many projects; and is far too limited a view about what counts as success for a project and its manager. End-dates and budgets are more often than not 'flexible.' If it were not so, the multitudes of projects that finish late and were grossly overspent would not be recognized as the successes they are.

To underscore this point—that despite what is claimed, time and budget are rarely significant constraints—look at the analysis of major

	Cost overrun		Actual traffic against forecast	
◆ Channel tunnel	An additional £4.80b	80%	18%	82% undershoot
○ Paris Nord, TGV	An additional £ 460m	25%	25%	75% undershoot

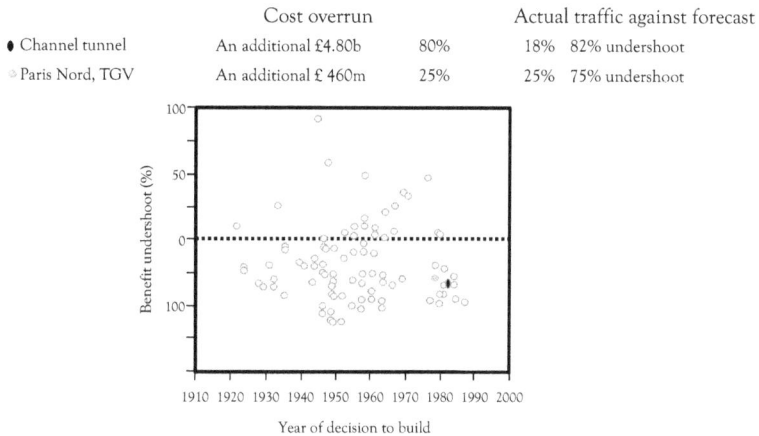

Figure 1.9 Overruns and underruns of time and cost

railway projects run over the past 70 years in various European countries and the United States, shown in Figure 1.9. (This data was collected by Flyvbjerg et al. (2003) who investigated the cost-benefit analyses of many major road and rail projects.) The vast majority overran their deadlines—and their budgets—often by well more than double, and occasionally by an order of magnitude. They also often magnificently failed to deliver the benefits that were promised. Most of these projects are considered a success, a significant contributor to their community, and to their country.

Analysis of decisions made, and the consequences incurred, shows that neither end-dates nor budgets were genuine constraints. At best, the values publicized were politicized estimates, and never did reflect the significant conditions for success for these projects. In these cases, the real success factor, the condition at the top of the decision tree, was the delivery to the key stakeholders' vision of what 'good looks like,' and if time and cost were factors at all, they were a long way down the list.

This brings us to a discussion about CSFs.

Critical Success Factors

Critical success factors are those things that must be present, and without which the project will fail. They are subject to special and continual management attention.

Consider the Sydney Opera House—late, late, late, and so overspent! During the project, the politicians were so incensed (and embarrassed) by the project that the architect was banished from Australia in perpetuity. Today the Opera House is regarded as an architectural triumph—one of the world's iconic buildings—and it put Sydney on the world's stage. What happened? For the Australian stakeholders, the condition of success was not project efficiency: meeting time, cost, and functionality. It was the impact that the project outcomes had on public opinion, the delivery of business success measured by corporate value, and, more tellingly, in terms of strategic potential—the societal value in the longer term. These conditions of success arise from stakeholder-driven CSFs.

There are three types of CSF. They can be categorized as temporal—there is a time criticality to be met; design—something about the design and approach to development that has to be satisfied; and stakeholder—an agenda of one or more of them that must be achieved. Table 1.3 shows examples of these three CSF types.

With more and more businesses using projects to achieve their strategic goals, the shift in emphasis in what makes a project successful toward the factors listed by Shenhar (1997) means that project managers

Table 1.3 Critical success factors examples

It is critical that:	Type of CSF
Registration is simple and convenient to the customer	**Design CSF:** specifying the acceptance criteria the 'registration' process *must* meet
The new applications interfaces to the existing SAP CRM	**Design CSF:** specifying acceptance criteria the new application *must* meet
Payment reminders for 'top up' are directly communicated to the customer in a timely way	**Design CSF:** additional products that *must* be provided to deliver top-up reminders
The game is ready for production by the 1st October to meet Christmas sales targets	**Temporal CSF:** indicates when the product *must* be delivered
The new IRT is acceptable to the taxi and bus associations	**Stakeholder CSF:** indicates which stakeholders' agendas *must* be addressed
No old documentation is in circulation post-D-Day—new documentation is only available after D-Day	A combination of **temporal and design CSFs**

must attend more closely to having the right impact and creating value. With the delivery of outputs being necessary but not sufficient to ensure project success, project managers must be concerned about CSFs as well as the constraints.

Planning a project is a goal-oriented process. The design of the plan is powerfully shaped by the constraints and CSFs imposed by the organization's business environment and management. The significance and impact of these on project planning are so profound that, depending on the priority of the constraints—where the constraint sits in the hierarchy of importance—the approach to planning changes. You can find an in-depth analysis of this, supported by project stories and examples in *Adaptive Project Planning* (Worsley & Worsley 2019).

Reflections

At the end of each chapter, we reflect on the chapter and pose questions for you to consider in light of your own experiences, your projects, and what makes them different. Taking time to give these some thought or better still discussing them with project colleagues back in your organization will, we believe, make the material more valuable to you.

In this chapter, we have described planning as modeling the real world to aid the project manager in transforming an understanding of what is wanted into a forecast of how to achieve it. The process of planning is crucial to all projects. How and if this gets translated into a physical plan is dependent upon the project context. The five functions of the plan are described as:

- The plan as a snapshot
- The plan as a map
- The plan as a communication
- The plan as engagement
- The plan as agreement

This chapter suggests that a plan should be physically composed of four different sections, with each section distinguished by its relative volatility.

Considering your own experience in running projects:

1. How well does your planning process address the five functions?
2. How are your plans structured? Any why? Is this mandated or a decision the project manager takes?
3. How do you capture changing project circumstances in your own plans? Are your plans good vehicles for dealing with volatility?
4. How and who sets the constraints on your project? What is the process to get a constraint changed?
5. Consider for a project you are involved with: What are the constraints and CSFs—who specified these?

CHAPTER 2

Goal-Oriented Planning

Focus on Purpose

A plan is a strategic document: a distillation of the many elements that set the project's identity. From it, it must be possible to determine the:

- *Purpose of the project*: the problem or opportunity it is addressing
- *Value of the project*: why is it worth doing–and to whom?
- *Objective*: what 'good looks like'–how you know the project has completed successfully
- *Scope*: what the project is expected to deliver in terms of physical things
- *Critical success factors*: what has to be in place for success
- *Risks*: what the main threats are to the success of the project

A good plan integrates these into a single coherent representation. Even the most complicated project can be planned in a document of no more than a few pages. Each distinct element has a role to play, but can only do so when kept separate. A common failing is to overload one of them, usually the objective. It becomes a hotchpotch of scope statements, activities, benefits and other outcomes, making it unsuitable for its role as the arbiter of best actions. We look at a few examples of unwieldy objectives later (see Table 2.2).

CITI developed the Project Mission Model™ (Figure 2.1) as a response to the relatively poor show made of planning projects. Its purpose is to structure the way stakeholders, project managers, and project management offices go about documenting plans.

The Project Mission Model™ explicitly distinguishes between the six views. (Impacts and benefits are two ways of setting out the value, and count as one.) The combination of the views related one-to-another

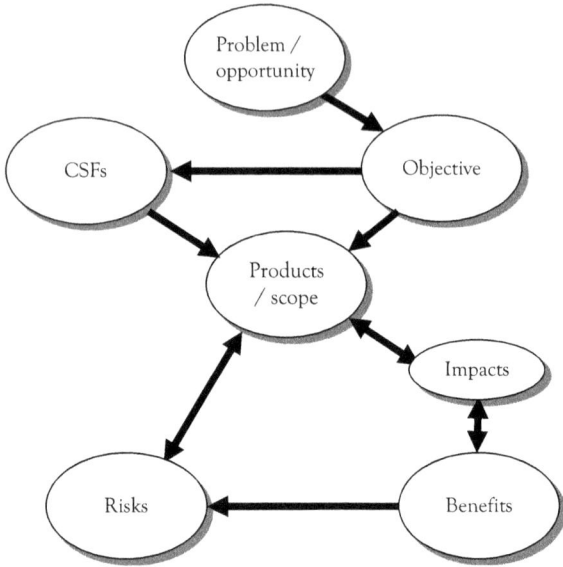

Figure 2.1 The Project Mission Model™

forms a holistic description of the project. Once developed, the analysis is translated into a one or two-page document, which we call the Project-on-a-Page, (abbreviated to POP). The template and an example are shown in Figure 2.2 and Table 2.1.

Planning can begin once there is an agreed POP. All the prerequisites are in place. How to go about completing the Project Mission

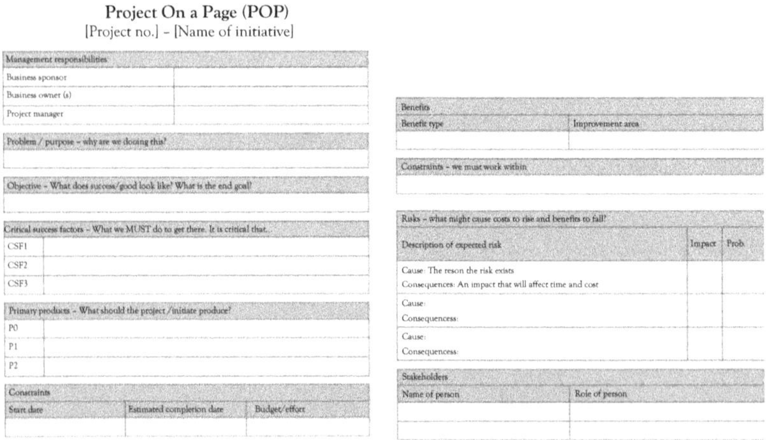

Figure 2.2 A project-on-a-page (POP) template

Table 2.1 **A completed project on a page (POP) example**

Project name	Management responsibilities	
Credit automation (2016/P543)	**IT sponsor**	Gail
	Business Sponsor	Heather
	Project Manager	Liesl

Problem/purpose
The effort associated with the current credit assessment and authorization processes means that we are not able to process all accounts satisfactorily and are unable to comply with internal credit control policies
The turn-around time for risk assessment is slow, subjective, and 'paper and mail dependent,' and difficult to follow through to the approval process. We cannot provide credit approval for customers quickly and safely, and business is frustrated due to the volume of order referrals. Turn-around times average 7 days and often much longer. Personnel are taking undue risks to ensure the company is positioned as the first choice supplier
Credit controllers manually identify accounts that they need to follow up on. The process is manual and time-consuming. Individual collection productivity is difficult to monitor, and there is no workflow functionality to queue and prioritize routine activities
Our query management process is non-existent. We cannot provide numbers in terms of value, nature, or the age of queries at short notice

Objective
Our financial services are regarded by our competitors as being best-in-class-credit management
Credit assessment and collections efforts are focused on the high return areas while low-concern accounts management is automated

Critical success factors–It is critical that:	
CSF1	Positive impacts on productivity are within acceptable time-scales
CSF2	The enhanced skills and behaviors of collections staff transform them from debt collectors to become credit relationship managers
CSF3	The online credit authorization process is best in class and used by authorized signatories

Primary products	
P0	Credit management, collections management, and dispute management modules
P1	XI/PI interfaces for the credit agency information
P2	Credit and dispute manager portal

Start date	**Estimated completion date**	**Budget/effort**
March	On hold	$2.8M

(*Continued*)

Table 2.1 (Continued)

Benefit type	Improvement areas
Cost avoidance	Reduce recruitment of staff to replace natural attrition ($3m) Reduction in the amount of provision made for bad debt ($1m)
Additional revenue	• Increase interest income ($1.9m) • Increase revenue from clients who would otherwise have spent elsewhere ($13m–profit: $0.7m)
Competitive advantage	Be easy to do business with: Faster turnarounds than competitors Better credit capabilities than competitors
Risk avoidance	Increase compliance with company policy and guidelines and NCA Reduce the risk of non-payment
Asset enhancement	Improve balance sheet
Risks	*Cause*: Managers continue to use existing MI from Excel-based sheets *Consequence*: Duplication of effort, incorrect behaviors rewarded

Model™ and its POP, and then do the planning is the subject of the rest of this chapter.

Focus on Outcomes

Let us look at the Project Mission Model™ as a tool. Somewhere, and somehow, an idea for a project has surfaced. To make the idea more concrete and to develop the basis for a motivation document three questions need to be answered. (The gray boxes in Figure 2.3.)

The Problem

Why is it being done? This first question is the proper starting point for any project. The answer should capture the purpose of the project. What is the problem that needs solving? Alternatively–and equally interesting–What opportunity is there that should be seized? What it should *not* be is a solution, even if it is dressed up as a problem. Running a project without knowing the underlying problem is certainly possible, many projects are, but it does put its successful completion in jeopardy.

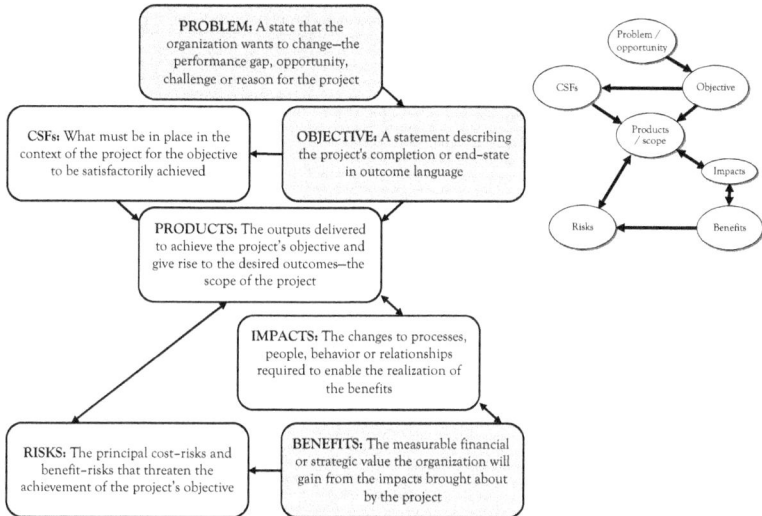

Figure 2.3 The Project Mission Model™—outcomes

The Benefits

Why is it worth doing? The second is also a why question, and there is always a subtext to it, which is: To whom is it valuable? Benefits are measurable additions of value to the organization and can be classified in several ways. One scheme, derived from work by Parker et al. (1988) is particularly elegant and uses eight categories split between financial and strategic classes:

Financial

- Cost avoidance (includes cost reduction)
- Additional income (from existing products, services or markets)
- New income (from new products, services or markets)
- Asset enhancement (making something more valuable for future financial gain)

Strategic

- Strategic alignment (developing capabilities required by the strategy)

- Competitive advantage (developing capability which threatens a competitor)
- Competitive response (developing a capability in response to a competitor's action)
- Intellectual property (developing capability as an asset–for future exploitation)

There is one other general justification for projects. Some projects do not deliver financial or strategically significant benefits but do contribute to the avoidance of risk, whether legal, financial, or reputational. Risk avoidance is not a benefit in the usual sense, as the organization is no better off after the project than before it–it's just not worse off, except for being poorer due to the expense of the project.

You might anticipate investors would have a clear understanding about the value of the return they expect from an investment. For projects, there is overwhelming evidence that this is not so. Benefits management remains in a woeful state. Benefits are confused with outcomes that may be wanted but have no value to the organization. They are often poorly identified, poorly quantified, and rarely deliberately managed. In many cases, benefits are claimed as a device to justify implementing a preferred solution, rather than as the basis for deciding which candidate projects to run.

The difficulty we experienced working with sponsors and stakeholders to express benefits led eventually to introducing the concept of 'impacts.' An impact is a change in state: of a product, a process, or a person's behavior–or indeed all three–regarded as useful or 'good' in some way. Impacts are always expressed as a comparative statement, comparing the 'now' with a preferred future state: it's faster, it's quicker, it's simpler, and so on. Impacts are caused by and directly attributable to the introduction of outputs or products into the organization's environment by a project. Impacts are not, in themselves benefits, though many benefit classification schemes confuse them with benefits. They are wanted, and when managed appropriately can result in delivering a recognized organizational benefit.

Figure 2.4 illustrates just a small part of the analysis of a large retail transformation program. You see the words used here in the impacts–called improvement areas by this company–'fewer,' 'more,' 'reduced,'

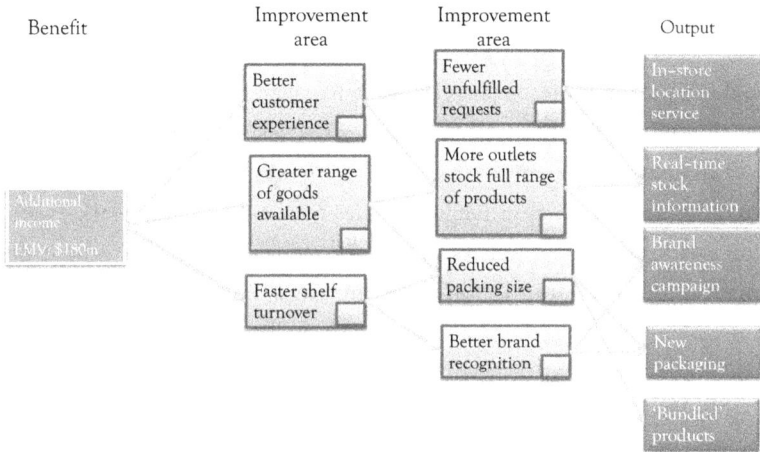

Figure 2.4 Linking benefits to impacts to outputs

and 'better,' *et cetera*. Each impact links directly to products delivered by, in this case, multiple projects. We find using terms such as impacts and improvement areas leads to much more fruitful conversations with the business stakeholders, and often is the beginning of a genuine commitment to the delivery of the changes. Using benefits, on the other hand, rarely triggers the same emotional response; 'cost avoidance,' and 'strategic alignment' does not seem to inspire the same level of personal responsibility.

The Objective

What does success looks like? This is the third question. The response should be a single statement describing the project's completion state framed in terms of changed organizational (and possibly personal) capabilities and relate directly to the problem or opportunity. It should not be a list of outputs delivered or services available; these are covered off elsewhere in the model. The purpose of the objective is to enable the sponsor, steering group, key stakeholders, and the project to test whether the desired state has been achieved and the project completed.

'SMARTing,' challenging the objective to see if meets the criteria of being: specific, measurable, achievable, realistic, and timely is a conventional technique for helping to refine objective statements. It can help to validate and improve the wording, but it is a terrible way of generating one. The ultimate test of a well-constructed objective is that the stakeholders and the project manager use it to make choices as to whether a decision or action will support achieving the desired end-state.

Generating clear, communicable objectives is not easy. Firstly, writing anything in concise, clear language takes time and is hard! Mark Twain, along with other great writers, is claimed to have said, "Sorry about the length of this letter, but I didn't have time to write a shorter one." When you find an analyst with the ability to actively listen and then replay what stakeholders mean in clear written prose, involve them in project initiation workshops (PIWs)–it will pay dividends!

Secondly, there is a tendency to want to include everything: making the objective into a portmanteau statement. Table 2.2 shows the original drafts of objective statements for three different projects; the problems with them; and then how they read after their PIWs. The following analysis shows some of the pitfalls to avoid:

- It is rarely the case that a project objective is best described as a list. Having multiple objectives can lead to awkward questions such as, "Which of these is the most important?" An objective that confuses is not helpful. Framing it as a single achievement is best. (Example 1 fails this test)
- An objective should *never* state what is going to be done. That is what a plan is for. It is a description of the desired end-state and so cannot be framed as an activity. Avoid verb-noun pairs, as they are 'doing' words. (Example 1 fails this test too!).
- Objectives that state or include some element of the solution are highly suspect. Is there a problem or opportunity, or is it just that someone wants his or her pet solution? If delivering a preferred solution is the real goal of the project, then so be it. That is a type of project; the solution has become a constraint, not an objective, and success means delivering the output, not the outcomes. (Example 2 suffers from this.)
- When the objective is a catchall for anxieties, benefits, and risks as well other thoughts about context and problems, there is a real issue about the preparedness of the organization

Table 2.2 Examples of the evolution of objective statements

	Example 1	Example 2	Example 3
Original	The objectives are to: • Develop theatre tool • Test the use of a centralized architecture • Order and install server(s) (if required) • Appoint and train requisite SME's • Deploy software • Train nursing staff • Capture data in hospital • Embed processes in all hospitals (change management) • User assessment and audit on use of the system • Sign off system per hospital	The objective is: OLEX has a single 'one-view' of every client. This 'one-view' is up to date, self-consistent, and reflects the knowledge that all client contact points in OLEX (sales representatives/account managers, call-center personnel, credit department, sales, and so on) has of the client.	Objectives and overview The responsibilities for the processing of pathology and radiology claims are shared; including being responsible for the adjudication and applying clinical rules. Any queries arising from these rules will be referred for resolution, and so on. The project has been broken down into four phases, as there will be a need for interface development for the full implementation of this service. The four phases are: And so on. (This objective was over a page in length)
What's gone wrong	The objective is a list of things to do or to deliver Objectives should be singular Completion of the project would mean the list has been completed, but what were the outcomes that were supposed to be achieved for the client?	The objective starts to identify the solution and acceptance criteria in the objective. 'And so on' is never acceptable in an objective and lists should be avoided. Which of the stakeholders this project had to satisfy turned out to be critical.	The objective and overview are conflated so there is no clear view of the end-state. Everything has been thrown into this section including the planning process!

(Continued)

Table 2.2 (Continued)

	Example 1	Example 2	Example 3
Post the workshop	The objective is: The capacity and skills requirements for a nursing team are based on its future roles, its training history, and on budgetary allocations	The objective is: The information held on clients by ESM key account managers is consistently and accurately captured in a central repository and is utilized to differentiate the quality and continuity of service provided to a client	The objective is: Every member in the group is treated equitably regarding access and comprehensibility of the scheme (All communications to be in members' preferred language)

to run the project at all. (Example 3 falls into this category. When the PIW concluded, the stakeholders were in turmoil. Was the initiative just a matter of translating the policies they sold into different languages?)

To get at the problem-objective-benefits side of the Project Mission Model™, the first one or two PIWs are for the key stakeholders. They need to engage. The project manager should attend, of course, and possibly other project team members, but they are observers, not contributors. Now is not their time.

It is quite likely you will find that despite the best efforts of a facilitator, the stakeholders will drift off into discussing solutions, their preferences, and even how to run the project, all of which is fine and should be recorded. However, the focus of these workshops is the outcomes; a domain wholly owned by the stakeholders, and is to determine what the project has to achieve. It's not that these other comments will be ignored; necessarily. As we will see, such comments by the stakeholders *may* be fundamental success criteria for the emerging project. So, all ideas should be captured in the appropriate place in the Project Mission Model™. These will be for discussion and review later.

The process of establishing answers to the three questions posed may take several iterations before everybody is happy with the wording. (See examples in Table 2.2.) We remember, with some delight, going through this process for a project in Ireland–it was the changeover to the Euro currency in a large bank. After a particularly tense workshop the sponsor, a senior manager in the bank commented, "To be sure, this clarity is a terrible thing." We like to think he meant it in a good way!

Focus on Outputs

With a good idea as to what it is that the stakeholders need from the project and hopefully their commitment, it is time to consider how to go about delivering it. Time for the second type of PIW, which requires technical and specialist input. Business stakeholders are always welcome, but rare. Solutionizing and optioneering are technical skills, establishing organizational needs and values are not, so the roles are reversed, and stakeholders become commentators rather than decision makers.

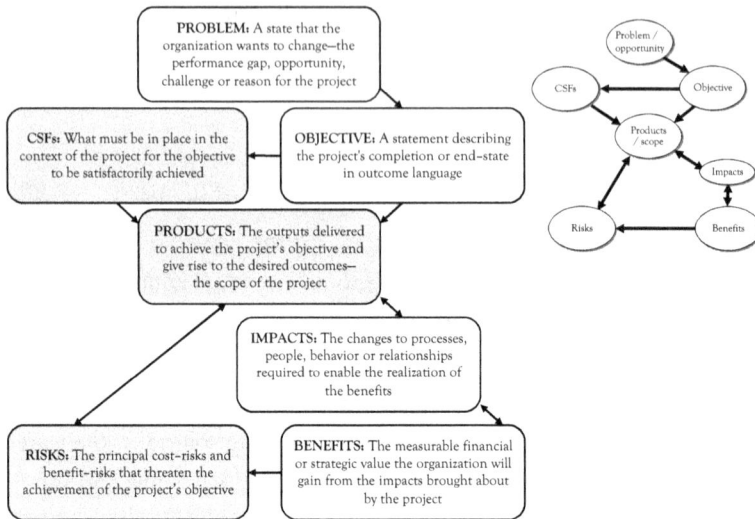

Figure 2.5 The Project Mission Model™—scoping

Looking at the Project Mission Model™ reproduced in Figure 2.5, we are now focusing on the grayed out boxes on the left-hand side of the model.

Products

What has to be produced? This is the central question for the project team. What is the project to build or buy to achieve the objective and cause the required impacts? At this level of planning, the focus is on the principal persistent products.

> *Persistent products or outputs*: Sometimes called deliverables, are what is left after the project is complete and which are instrumental in causing the outcomes (impacts and benefits) expected from the project.

The objective is not the only source to consider when identifying products or outputs. In total, there are four sources, and together they establish the scope of the project. Inspection of Figure 2.5 shows four arrowheads pointing to the 'PRODUCTS' box.

In many projects, the management of risk can generate a substantial number of additional products. These arise, for example, from the need to protect the outputs from defects–products made necessary by quality assurance and control processes. Many are temporary but are still essential to the delivery of a successful project.

Temporary or non-persistent products: exist in two forms:

- *Interim products* necessarily created as part of the development process—such as requirements, designs, test rigs *et cetera*—but that do not form part of the delivered output.
- *Management products* to communicate the project planning process and the performance of the project. Typical management products are project status reports, test results, and similar documents.

It is also common for critical success factor analysis to identify the need for additional products. In the case of stakeholder-sensitive and stakeholder-led projects, communications products may be more than 50 percent of the total scope.

The fourth source is from impacts. More common in projects found in programs than independent projects (see Chapter 5), the need for such additional products arises because necessary changes of behavior would not otherwise be supported.

Risks

What could cause costs to rise or the value of benefits to fall? At this level of planning the focus is on the 'big hairy' risks. As we will see later, risk analysis features as a continuing thread in all planning. For now, it is necessary to expose, share, and agree with the stakeholders what risks ought to be factored into the planning process right from the start.

A *risk* is any potential event that could have a negative impact on achieving the objective or outcomes of a project, and, which you *intend to manage*.

A plan must identify the risks and their likely impact. Risks that affect the way the project is executed are the province of the project manager and are called cost-risks, principally because they almost always cause the costs to rise in some way. Risks that affect the achievement of the benefits are termed benefit-risks. Responsibility for these lies with the project sponsor, which may be why they are so often undermanaged. Project planning needs to recognize both types.

Risks, even at this early stage, should be listed in the project risk log. The sources of risks identified at this stage will usually be associated with the products, the benefits, and specific stakeholders. Sources of risk often overlooked at this stage are those threats to the organization that arise in the circumstance that the project does successfully complete and provide the outputs and outcomes it promised. Even success comes with its own risks!

Critical Success Factors

What has to be right? The third question this workshop needs to answer is often the hardest, and as we will see, can have a profound influence on the conduct of the project and its planning. As with the previous two questions, CSFs are in many cases derivative and can be identified by analysts, as they often arise from analysis of the assertions made in the objective and benefit statements. Every CSF is determined and owned by the project stakeholders. We mentioned in the early PIWs, driven by the stakeholders, that what is said may later become incorporated in the Project Mission Model™. This is why. When stakeholders make assertions about solutions and impacts they want, as opposed to need, they may be describing, albeit in code, some of their CSFs.

Projects typically have between two and eight project-specific CSFs. It is vital to test that they are necessary. A simple test is to check that the project will definitely *fail* if they are not met. The second and more useful one is to establish what additional management actions need to be taken to achieve the CSF. If the only management actions you can take are those you are already taking as part of the standard project management process, then the CSF identified is generic. In which case, there is no need to list it or to manage it. Let's look at a couple of examples.

Example 1: A colleague argues "It is critical that the requirements are correctly captured" is a project CSF. Of course, it is because if you don't get them right, the project can't be a success. When, however, you look for project management actions that you aren't already taking, there aren't any. This is a generic CSF. The appropriate management should already be in place. There is nothing more to be done. Establishing the right requirements may be hard, it may go wrong, but it is not a risk, it's a generic critical success factor–something you should always expect to manage for.

Example 2: "Unless Trevor–a specific and talented resource–is part of the project team the project will fail." If Trevor is a critical resource, then this is a CSF, and I'm sure most project managers have faced a situation like this. A review of the plan makes it obvious that several additional management actions could be taken to secure Trevor: You might decide to take his line manager out for lunch. Perhaps, you could make a series of agreements and undertakings; to be sure he is made available to your project. These actions you would be unlikely to contemplate unless having access to Trevor was a CSF. But as access to Trevor *is* a project-specific CSF, these actions must be an integral part of your project plan and claim their share of your management attention. What they are not are contingent risk management actions, which they would be if the non-availability of Trevor were treated as a mere risk.

What both examples have in common is that it makes no sense to treat a CSF as if it was a risk. A CSF is a no-fail condition. You need to put all the necessary and sufficient actions in place to ensure the CSF else the project will fail. So, if there is a management action that can be taken, it should be *in* the project plan, not in a risk plan.

Reflections

In this chapter, we have focused on the development of the strategic aspects of a project's plan, capturing the stakeholders' perspectives on the outcomes and the scope of the project.

These are the big ideas we would like to leave you with:

- Plans that are not linked to business outcomes are a significant cause of project failure
- Planning is never done alone

- The perfect plan does not exist. Your goal is to model reality as usefully, not as closely, as possible
- If doing the planning isn't hard, you probably aren't doing it right.

The Project Mission Model™ is used by us at four points during a project's life cycle.

(a) At the moment when the project motivation document is in the process of being drawn up
(b) Just before planning starts in earnest
(c) About three-quarters of the way through the planning phase
(d) At project closedown

The revisiting at points (b) and (c) are to ensure that as the understanding about the project increases this is captured in the mission statement, and where necessary the wording is redrafted with the close cooperation of the stakeholders. The review at project closedown is a specific communication process to ensure that there remains a close alignment between what the project says it has delivered and what the stakeholders understand has been delivered.

Considering your own experience in running projects:

1. If you had to coach a novice project manager on how to produce a project plan, how would go about doing that? Do you have a preferred approach?
2. Does the organization mandate that you use document templates for motivation documents, business cases, and plans? What do you consider are the advantages of using a planning template? Are there any disadvantages in your experience?
3. When reporting your project, do any of the members of the project board ask about the critical success factors of the project, and what has been done in the previous period to address them? Do you?

4. How do you set out the scope for your project? Do you identify aspects that are to be excluded? What is the basis for that exclusion? Do you consider them to be design constraints?
5. Do you routinely try to establish and document the reasons why the project has been established? How often is the purpose of the project to deliver a pre-specified solution?

CHAPTER 3

The Process of Planning

The six views have been captured. What the world is to be like at the end of the project is understood, and why it is important to succeed, as well as what it is worth and to whom. In most cases, the basis for the solution is also agreed. All there is left to do is to ensure that the money and effort expended is structured, sequenced, and demonstrably connected back to the desired outcomes. So the next stage is to work out how to provide the outputs, what tasks to perform, by whom, and in what order.

Figure 3.1 shows an amended Project Mission Model™ that takes into account the factors needed to convert the strategic aspects of the project into a tactical plan. There is a crucial link—a bridge—maintained between the outputs and structuring the project effort.

The bridge makes it possible for a plan to serve the stakeholder community of the project and the project team. If the link is broken project execution becomes detached from the purpose, and expectation management is blinded. What occurs over the bridge is the translation of what is wanted into how to get it done.

You will have noticed the Project Mission Model™ is now framed by two fundamental planning elements. We have already discussed constraints and their role in planning, how they shape the planning process, and determine the validity of a plan.

Assumptions are those things held to be true for the purpose of project planning and management.

The other is assumptions. We will discuss their role in planning in more detail in the section on logs in the following section. For now, it is enough to know that plans are very vulnerable to the set of assumptions made. When an assumption proves to be invalid, the project manager has

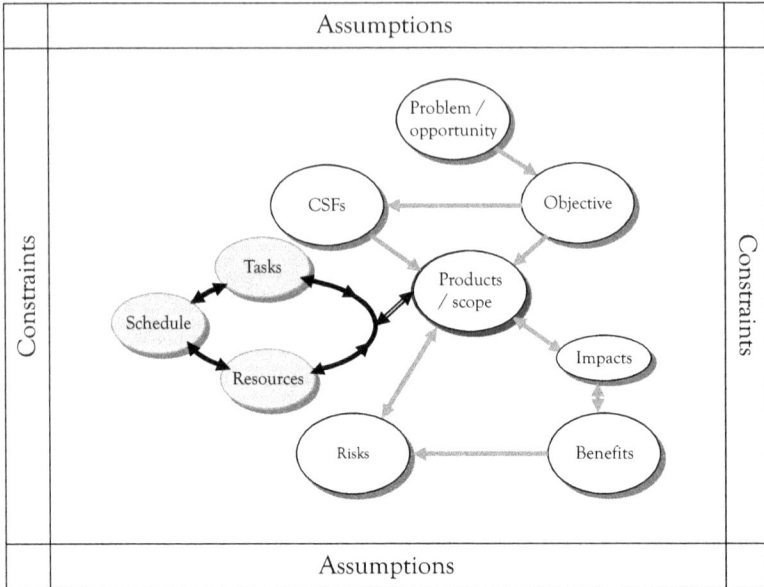

Figure 3.1 The full project mission model™

to re-plan using different assumptions, and the stakeholders need to be made aware of what has happened.

Steps from Constraints to Resources

The steps to formulating the project plan are: *First determine the…*

Products—the outputs you need to achieve the outcomes: *Then look at the…*

Processes—tasks that will get you these products: *This will suggest the types of…*

Resources—capabilities needed for the tasks: *These three aspects each can create…*

Risks—that threaten the achievement of the objective: *These four integrate into a…*

Schedule—activities with resources sequenced: *And all together must meet…*

Stakeholder—expectations: It is their view that determines whether a plan is acceptable.

The sequence of steps is easy to remember. It is 'C' followed by an alphabetic stammer:

C—Constraints
P—Products (outputs)
P—Processes (tasks)
R—Resources
R—Risks
S—Schedule
S—Stakeholders

There is a temptation to see planning as being a top-down process, done in a single pass. This is most decidedly not the case! As Figure 3.2 shows, each step can cause you to go back, to revisit choices and decisions made higher up the chain. The two immovable things—the only two things project managers cannot change—are the constraints and the objective. They have to get permission from the sponsor and other key stakeholders to change either of those otherwise they are in very real danger of damaging that crucial link, the bridge, between the Project Mission Model™ and the executable plan.

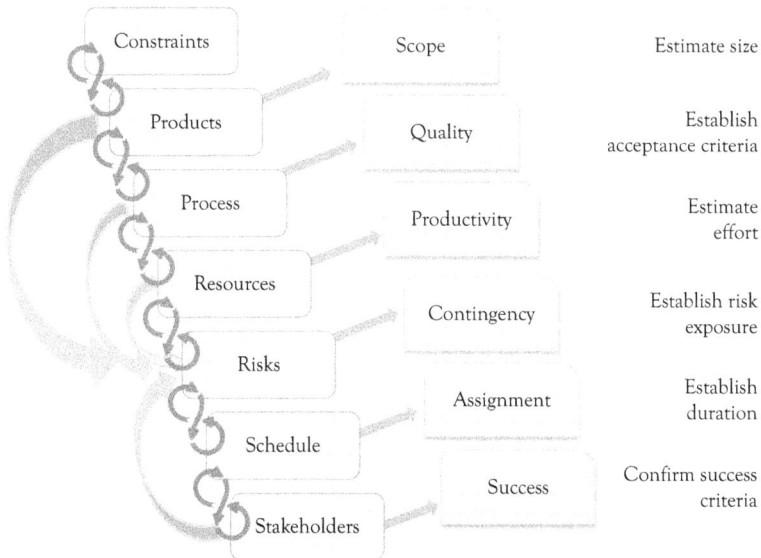

Figure 3.2 The basic planning steps and their associated knowledge areas

So planning is a process. Naturally, there are variants, but the basic sequence is captured by 'CPPRRSS.' Step one establishes the 'box' in which the plan has validity—what are the constraints the project, and hence the plan, must work within. For some projects, it might be that the fundamental constraint is that the project must deliver the complete functionality specified. For others, it may be that the project must be ready by 1 January. While for others, it's that there is no more than $100,000 available to spend.

I know you'll tell me that all three have to be met. A quick thought experiment, however, suggests otherwise. Most of the time, one is going to prove to be the most important. When it comes to a trade-off, one will consistently be chosen above the others. As discussed in Chapter 1, there is always a hierarchy although it may not immediately be apparent which one is on top. Sponsors and stakeholders are not always clear in their own minds as to what is truly important. Sometimes the only way to establish what the real constraints are is by engaging with them during planning, by posing situations and seeing how issues are resolved. If you base your planning on a wrong assumption about what's at the top of their list, it will quickly become obvious!

The next step involves elaborating on the outputs or products. You should avoid identifying the processes at this stage. Many project managers mistakenly go immediately to structure the work into tasks and activities. Projects are a vehicle for producing products—or outputs. That's what they do—in fact that's about all they do! To be a successful project manager, you must know what the project is going to produce: what you will buy, what you will build.

Discussing tasks before knowing what the outputs are is usually a grievous error. So list the outputs! You won't get them all, and you will not get them all right—but it's a great beginning, and something you can easily check with the stakeholders. Facing them with things rather than technical processes and tasks makes it much easier to make decisions. Once you have a list of the set of products, you will have definitively established the scope of the project—a great basis for planning.

Start by agreeing what the principal persistent products (those outputs that will remain after the project has closed) should be. This will be, for the most part, what the project must deliver to meet its objectives.

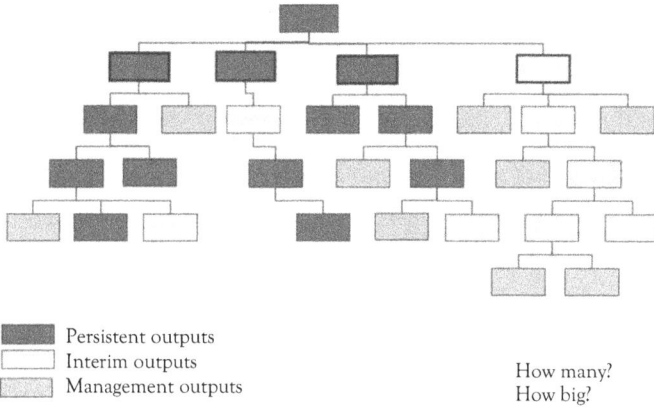

Persistent outputs
Interim outputs
Management outputs

How many?
How big?

Figure 3.3 A product breakdown structure (PBS)

This list, which began life in the POP, can be developed as a product breakdown structure (PBS), see Figure 3.3.

> The PMBOK (2013) uses the term WBS, standing for work breakdown structure, instead of PBS. Our view is that this was an early PMI misnomer, which once made they felt unable to correct. The definitions of the WBS entries, that they must be nouns; that each element is a deliverable are worthy, but even their own examples include ambiguities. Saying a deliverable is a 'door painted' is just a way of sneaking in an activity! We suspect the deliverable is a 'door' with associated acceptance criteria such as the color should be appropriate; it should be weatherproof, and so on. To confuse things even more, the 6th edition of the PMBOK (2018) now explicitly encourages 'work to be performed' entries to feature in the deliverable-oriented decomposition.
>
> We strongly recommend the separation of products from tasks, deliverables from work activities and so use PBS to set out the products, and WBS to lay out the work to be done. It just seems a more natural use of the language!

While developing the PBS, estimates of how many and how big each of the products is likely to be should be made. These should reflect the level of uncertainty by using a ranged estimate rather than a single-value guess. Once you've set out the outputs, and this may involve several iterations, it is now appropriate to define the tasks (methods, techniques, and tools) to acquire (create or purchase) each product. As you are doing so, it is also important to establish the level of quality—the acceptance criteria (ACs)—that the stakeholders expect. The ACs are usually negotiable, unlike constraints and CSFs. By establishing the ACs now, the likely processes, as well as the likelihood and type of defects to expect, can be determined.

In *Adaptive Project Planning* (Worsley and Worsley 2019), we discuss whether and when decisions about the underlying product development life cycle should be made part of the planning. For now, it is enough to note that these decisions may have contractual implications under certain procurement models and will usually specify the quality management system as well as any overarching standards that demand compliance.

The task list, which can be organized into a logical work breakdown structure (WBS), is not yet sequenced. Best practice is to keep the PBS and the WBS as distinct elements, as is strongly encouraged by PRINCE2®. However, many methods (and the PMI) allow or even promote both products and tasks to be defined in a single structure, confusingly called a WBS.

Once the WBS is created, estimates of skill and likely resource demand can be made. These, too, should reflect the level of uncertainty and be provided as ranged estimates.

A *ranged estimate* is where two values: an optimistic and a pessimistic value is given, and the range represents the level of uncertainty that exists about the actual value. Estimates have different sources of uncertainty. Consider the case where you are asked to estimate the number of marbles in a jar. If the jar is actually full of marbles you could make a correct guess, and check your answer by counting the marbles. However, in projects, when you estimate, you are being asked how many marbles *could* there be in the jar when the jar is in fact empty, so there is no 'right' answer, you cannot count them—there aren't any in the jar!

An accurate ranged estimate is one that includes the number of marbles that are in the event, found in the jar. A good ranged estimate is one in which the range suggested is relatively narrow and includes the 'discovered' value.

There is a view that there is no such thing as a single-valued 'estimate.' People who respond with one are not estimating, they are just guessing. A view we whole-heartedly agree with!

The effort required is *derivative* of the number and size of each product set out in the PBS. The effort demand can be modeled in yet another breakdown structure—one that reflects the resource structure of the organization—an OBS. The choice of process inevitably dictates the kind of resource you need—the skill sets necessary to carry out the process.

Steps from Risks to Stakeholders

So, we have now considered 'CPPR'—the constraints, products, processes, and resources. The next 'R' is the set of risks. As you step through the planning process you will identify risks: risks from the products (level of performance), risks from the processes chosen (types of defects arising), and risks from the resources (capability and productivity) you are going to use. The arrows in Figure 3.2 indicate this. Can you deal with these risks? Does each risk have an owner? Does each risk have a set of management actions to allow you to manage the likelihood of occurrence or impact on the project's objective of the risk? Can your project handle that level of risk exposure? Are your stakeholders prepared to accept it? If not, you do not have a viable plan—you are going to have to iterate.

Now, and only now, are you in a position to devise the schedule— the sequence with which your project is going to order the tasks and activities, and when to engage the various resources. Without a doubt, the appropriate scheduling of effort time within calendar time is what distinguishes good project managers from less capable ones—it is a fundamental skill. It is also, however, secondary to and derivative of the planning process.

Scheduling is the conversion of the project plan into a timetable—the schedule. Now, while plans are strategic and owned by the governance group, schedules are tactical and owned by the project manager. Unlike plans, which are relatively stable unless basic assumptions prove invalid, schedules are highly volatile. So when producing a schedule, schedule the 'next stage' in detail, with more distant events only identified by milestones. There is far too high a level of uncertainty to justify the cost of detailed scheduling for tasks months in the future.

What constitutes a 'stage' of a project is a decision made by the project manager. The stage may be a set of activities with well-defined outputs such as 'analysis' or 'design.' Alternatively, it could be a management device to exercise control over a complex set of activities. Whatever the case, one thing is sure; it makes no sense to schedule at a level of detail than you cannot control, or out much beyond three months. This means that scheduling changes from being a 'fire and forget' activity, and becomes instead at least a weekly or fortnightly interaction.

Typically, schedules are based on the WBS, and it is good practice to create work packages—sets of tasks with their resources—for each primary deliverable. With this approach, it is vital that dates in those sub-schedules are coordinated with the master schedule, and that the master schedule is coordinated with the business milestones within the overall project plan. The project manager's responsibility is to insist on and maintain this consistency. The actual scheduling of the task and work packages may be delegated to work package managers—once the project manager has established and checked appropriate due dates.

Schedules create project risk. The partitioning and sequencing of tasks, allocating activities to resources, the degree of parallelism of tasks, creating high fan-outs, and high fan-ins, (see Figure 3.4) are project-scheduling decisions that cause and carry project risk.

So there you have it. All the technical aspects of planning set out in a step-by-step process. However, we are not yet finished! There is one more 'S' to factor into the plan—and it can be a game-changer.

This final factor may invalidate all that you've done so far—and you may have to reiterate the whole plan. This last 'S' is the stakeholders. We started with business stakeholders right at the beginning of the Project Mission Model™ process, as they are the ones who have to supply the view

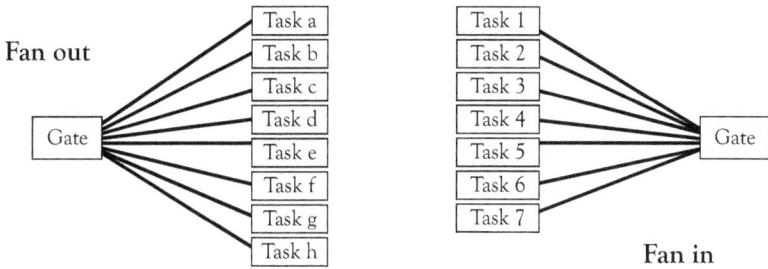

Figure 3.4 Risks created by scheduling

as to the outcomes. Now a broader group of stakeholders has to be consulted. The crucial test the plan must survive is whether the various solutions, trade-offs and tactical considerations made, meet the stakeholders' needs and expectations. If it does, you have a viable plan; if it does not, the plan will have to be changed. You have to ask, and you have to listen. Your solution may be good—it may even be technically perfect—but it is their possibly political, possibly erroneous, perspectives that matter. It may be sad, it may even from your project manager standpoint, be senseless, but it is nevertheless true that they are the arbiters of success—and being a professional project manager means you had better heed it.

This final point has an enormous impact on the approach to planning. The plan is not yours. It is not primarily for the project manager, it is for the stakeholders, and in particular for the needs of those stakeholders that form the governance group for the project. This has all sorts of consequences, from determining the plan's contents, the appropriate format, to the level of detail it should go to, and the communication needs it has to address.

So, that's nearly it for planning many straightforward projects. There is just one more topic to discuss. How do the constitutive elements of a plan sitting in the logs affect and modify the planning activity and management?

The Role of Logs in Planning

As a plan is a model of that part of the world we want to manipulate or control, a good plan should provide quick access to every factor and force that by their interplay affect the achievement of the goal. The format that best provides this for most of these factors is a set of prioritized, inter-linked, and annotated lists.

There are two commonly used techniques to construct such lists. One, we've already discussed briefly: the structured breakdown. Examples of breakdown structures are the PBS, the WBS, and the organizational breakdown structure (OBS). They are useful visual tools as they are more supportive than simple lists in checking for the three "C"s of coherence, consistency, and completeness.

The use of 'logs' is the other technique. Most project managers have come across the use of logs, typically in the form of a risk log, or a risk and issue log, but they are often misused, being little more than a recording mechanism rather than a vital resource in the process of planning and executing a project.

First, let us set out for the record that every project should have nine logs as part of its plan. Each log should be set up at project initiation and should be the only place where what it records is recorded. As a simple example, there should a single place where risks, as they are identified or discovered, are recorded. This risk log is a crucial part of the project, and yet it is a widespread practice to record risks within the body content of different project documents. Often these risks are not carried forward consistently as the planning process elaborates the detail, moving from project initiation to project brief to project plan. Some are lost, some morph, new ones arise, and there is no overview or 'big picture.' Such a loss! And it's not limited to risks. It is true for all nine of them.

The nine logs we recommend to be set up are stakeholders, assumptions, constraints, changes, risks, issues, dependencies, decisions, and agreed and minuted actions. What makes these planning components suitable candidates for being in a log is that each has a lifecycle. There is a moment when it becomes recognized, a period when it is active and requires management attention, and a point where it is no longer relevant. Each has associated attributes such as ownership, linked management actions, and a period during which they could affect the project. Figure 3.5 illustrates a number of examples of some of the logs.

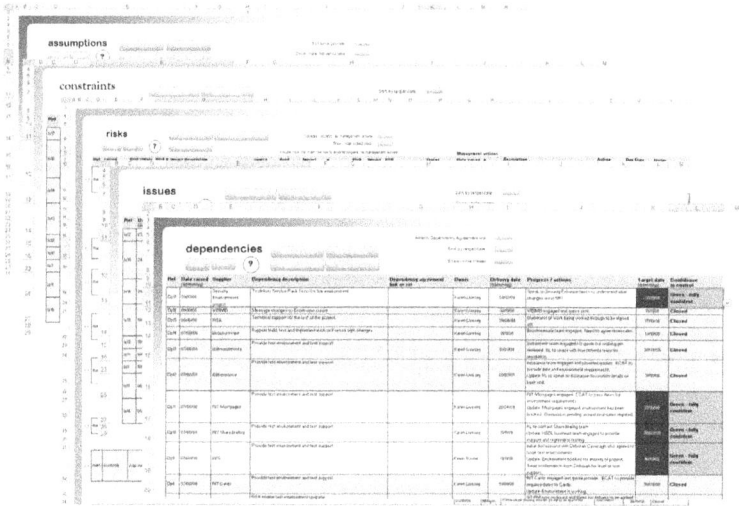

Figure 3.5 Examples of some project logs

There are many suggestions in the literature for the structure of the various logs (we've included some on the website associated with this book). Increasingly we see Enterprise Project Office systems become the single source of log information. This approach has several advantages, it:

- Encourages the standard use of logs across the project community
- Avoids the duplication of risks inconsistently recorded across documents
- Provides a source for portfolio-wide analysis, with perhaps the most widespread use being to collate, report on, and highlight common risks and issues.

Another benefit of the approach is that the central repository makes it easier for the project office to review the quality of the logging process.

In this section, we are going to look in a little more detail at some of the most commonly used logs and the linkages and relationships that exist between risks, issues, assumptions, constraints, dependencies, and the CSFs of a project.

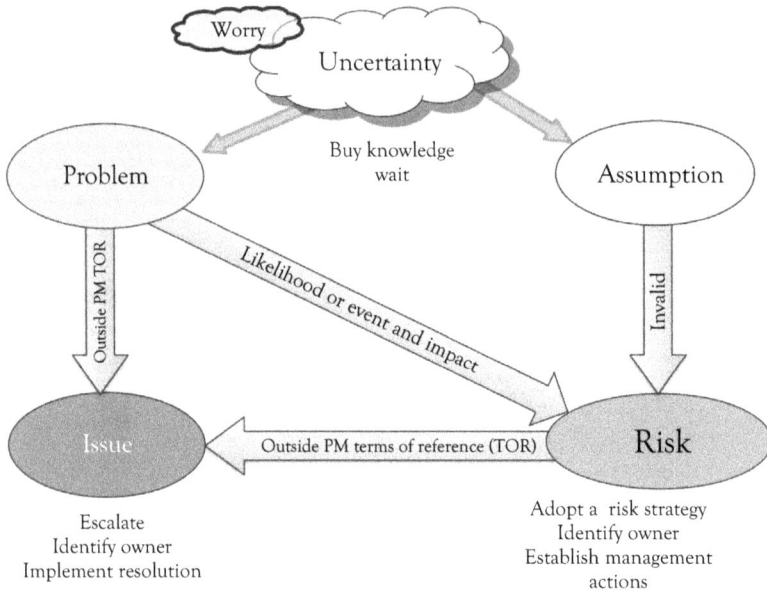

Figure 3.6 Relationships between some planning constitutive elements

There is much unhelpful confusion between these elements, and this can lead to poor planning. Figure 3.6 illustrates the ways in which some of these are related to each other. Let us start by sorting out the relationships between assumptions, risks, issues, and problems.

First a few definitions, then a discussion as to why keeping the distinctions clear helps.

Assumptions

What an assumption is has already been defined as being something held to be true, usually for planning purposes. It may not be true, and indeed the planner may not even believe it to be true, but there is nothing in the definition that says it has to be true, just that it is held to be true in order to develop a feasible plan. The only management action associated with an assumption—other than logging it—is to monitor the assumption to check that it remains a valid assertion. Logging assumptions require little

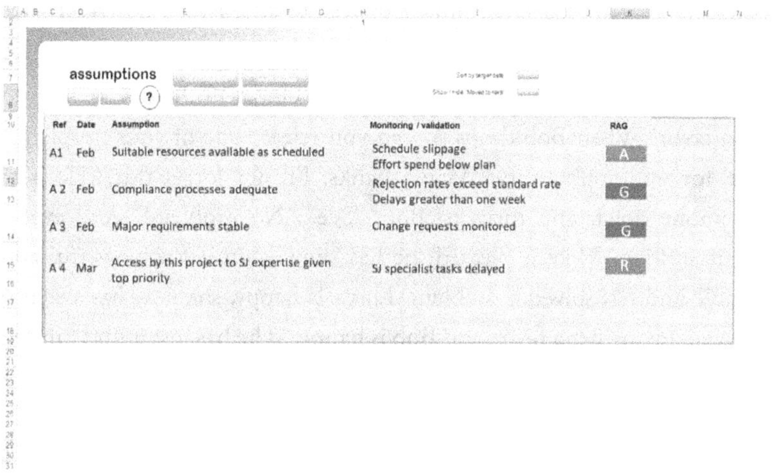

Ref	Date	Assumption	Monitoring / validation	RAG
A1	Feb	Suitable resources available as scheduled	Schedule slippage Effort spend below plan	A
A 2	Feb	Compliance processes adequate	Rejection rates exceed standard rate Delays greater than one week	G
A 3	Feb	Major requirements stable	Change requests monitored	G
A 4	Mar	Access by this project to SJ expertise given top priority	SJ specialist tasks delayed	R

Figure 3.7 An example of an assumption log

effort; see Figure 3.7 for an example entry. We'll discuss later what to do if the monitoring indicates that the assumption is no longer valid.

Issues

Projects are awash with problems. It is one of the reasons that there is a project manager and why they are the single point of accountability for accomplishing the project's objective. Most project problems are the province of project managers, who may make use of others to help resolve them, but the problems are in their sphere of control.

An *issue* is a problem that is outside the remit of the project manager to solve.

There are, however, some problems that project managers are not authorized to address, and to do so would be exceeding their brief: these are correctly identified as issues. Let's look at how this plays out in a typical project setting.

A project manager, we'll call him Bob, is having difficulty obtaining the resources he needs. People promise him support, but it does not materialize. So, he raises this as an issue with his sponsor. His sponsor, a supportive type, we'll call him Mike, listens patiently and then says, "No problem, let me fix this for you." Mike picks up the phone and says to Linda, a manager of suitable resources, "Linda, hi there. Can you do me a favor? When Bob drops by can you release one of your people for him, for me? You're a star. Many thanks. I'll not forget this." He puts the phone down and turns to Bob, "See... No problem!" And everyone is smiling. Mike is pleased; he has shown himself as powerful and capable and has solved a problem. Linda is happy, she now has a senior manager owing her a favor, and Bob is happy, as he has just found himself a resource manager for his project! As for project management and its planning disciplines—the whole scene is a bit of a disaster.

Not being able to secure the resources the plan calls for is definitely a problem. In fact, it is probably the commonest problem in projects, but it is not an issue—at least not yet. There are many routes available to Bob to solve his problem; including restructuring the work to avoid the use of what may well be a scarce resource.

While Bob's attempt to use his sponsor to solve his resource problem demonstrates his lack of experience as a project manager, Mike's acceptance of it as an issue is inexcusable. Bob's inability to solve the resource problem—his apparent incompetence—might well be an issue. Mike might like to focus on that. However, acting as Bob's resource manager will lead to a transfer of responsibility and an increase in involvement and workload for the sponsor. This is something many sponsors complain about, but which, like Mike, they bring upon themselves.

We need to complete this story because there are some circumstances in which Bob's predicament may genuinely be an issue and not just his problem. Consider the case that the priority of Bob's project is considered by some resource owners to be so low as not to warrant resourcing. Other candidate projects are more deserving in their eyes. In this circumstance, the observed behaviors might be the same, but the problem is different and is not one that Bob, or any project manager, could resolve. This is now about the lack of political will to execute this project among a number of the key stakeholders.

Now the problem is one of insufficient priority. This is an issue. Only the sponsor has the remit to deal with this problem. Every issue, like every risk, must have an owner—but unlike risks that the owner cannot be the project manager. Figure 3.8 shows an example of an issue log and the attributes that are commonly held with an issue statement.

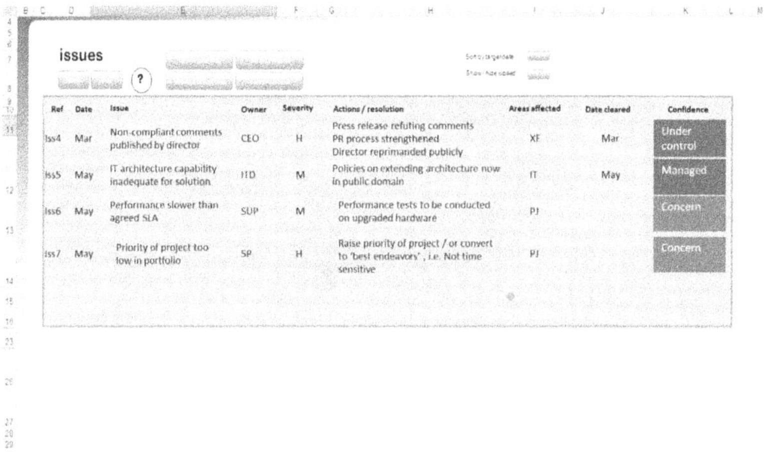

Ref	Date	Issue	Owner	Severity	Actions / resolution	Areas affected	Date cleared	Confidence
Iss4	Mar	Non-compliant comments published by director	CEO	H	Press release refuting comments PR process strengthened Director reprimanded publicly	XF	Mar	Under control
Iss5	May	IT architecture capability inadequate for solution	ITD	M	Policies on extending architecture now in public domain	IT	May	Managed
Iss6	May	Performance slower than agreed SLA	SUP	M	Performance tests to be conducted on upgraded hardware	PJ		Concern
Iss7	May	Priority of project too low in portfolio	SP	H	Raise priority of project / or convert to 'best endeavors', i.e. Not time sensitive	PJ		Concern

Figure 3.8 An example of an issue log

Project managers not only confuse issues with project problems but also confuse issues with risks. The number of times we've read on a risk log: "There are insufficient resources on the project" is nearly as many as the number of risk logs we've analyzed, and that's many hundreds. How can this be a risk? If it is true then it is a current state of affairs, it has already happened, so it is an issue, if unsolvable by the project manager. There is no uncertainty, which brings us to the next log, risks.

Risks

To be valuable in the planning process, it is crucial to distinguish risks from worries, and, from opportunities. (There has been a move to conflate risk with opportunity. Although an apparent symmetry does exist between these two concepts, by confusing risk management with opportunity management, the planning utility of regarding risk as a hazard is reduced. The professional bodies have done a disservice to its practitioners and in our mind should reconsider.)

In project management, a risk has three components, each of which must be logged before it can be correctly identified as a risk. The first is the *cause.* (In several models of risk, the cause is called the 'event.') The cause should be less than 50 percent likely to occur. If it is more-likely-than-not to occur, planning should assume it would happen. A plan should set out what to expect and how to react in circumstances that are likely to exist, and proceed on that basis.

A *risk* is anything that *may* happen which would threaten the achieving of the project's objective.

A risk has three components:

- the *cause or event* that will give rise to the threat to the objective
- the *consequence or impact* being the negative impact the event will give rise to
- the *set of management actions* taken to address the event or the impact or both.

The second component is the *consequence*. To be considered a risk, any impact must reduce the likelihood of achieving the project's objective within the set of constraints set for the project. (This gives rise to the idea that there are two classes of risk: those that affect the execution of the project itself, which we call cost-risks, and those that reduce the value of the project outcomes, which we call benefit-risks.)

The third component is the set of management actions taken to address the risk. Without associated management actions, the purported risk is nothing more than a worry. The project governance group: project manager and steering group, has in effect made an assumption that the cause will not occur, with all the consequences in terms of responsibility, liability, and unpreparedness that comes with that decision. (Remember an assumption is something held to be true for planning purposes, and the only management action is monitoring.). Figure 3.9 provides a couple of example entries in a risk log.

When deciding on the management actions, it is necessary to determine who will own the risk as this may alter both what will be done, and by whom. Unlike issues, the owner can be the project manager, and very often is.

Though the possible management actions are legion, they can be categorized into just five basic strategies. The classification emerges from considering whether the management action will be taken before or after the event has occurred, and whether the action is aimed at the managing the event (cause), or the impact (consequence). The illustration in Figure 3.10 should help to make this clear. The five strategies are:

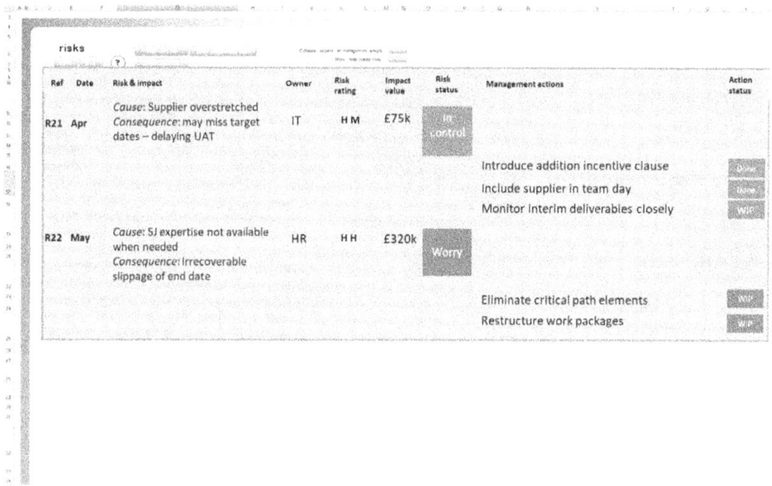

Figure 3.9 An example of a risk log

- *Avoid* the event leading to a negative impact
- *Reduce* the likelihood of the event happening
- *Transfer* the risk to someone better able to cope with it
- *Protect* the project against (some of) the negative consequences of the impact
- *Make good* the effect of the impact—fix-on-failure

You may notice there is no mention of 'accepting the risk' as a risk management strategy. When it is claimed the risk has been accepted, the reality is that an assumption has been made that it's not going to happen, a situation rapidly altered when the assumption proves to be invalid, and the management action that then follows is 'fix-on-failure.'

Let's consider the situation where you are offered the opportunity to drink from a fizzy drink can that fell out of the bag and down a flight of stairs. There is a problem: fizzy drinks cans are aerated and shaking them before opening is likely to cause you to be sprayed and you would lose a good portion of the drink. So, the event is opening an agitated can, the consequences are you don't get the drink you want, and perhaps getting soaked—so what are your possible management actions?

Avoidance is one strategy. You could avoid the risk by finding something else to drink.

Reduction of the likelihood of the event is another strategy. There are several options here. You could wait a few hours for the gas to be re-dissolved, or you could try the dubious trick of flicking the can's side to reduce outgassing. The approach is to find a way of reducing the likelihood of the explosive release of gas and liquid when the can is opened.

Transferring the risk to someone else is also a feasible option. If you give the can, and the problem, to someone else, perhaps someone who knows better than you do how to degas the can safely, or who has ways of dealing with being soaked, you can get the job done. Many projects adopt transfer as a risk strategy when they contract specialists to do a particular piece of work for them—exchanging a risk they can manage (higher costs) for a risk they cannot.

Each of these risk management strategies is designed to manage the risk by addressing the likelihood of the event occurring. There are two further strategies, which deal with the consequences.

Protection against the worst of the consequences, in other words reducing the significance of the impact, is one sensible strategy. It means incurring effort and cost before the event of course. In this situation, you might decide to acquire a mac or have purchased some plastic bags and open the can under a cover, capturing the lost liquid and protecting yourself from being sprayed.

Finally, there is the commonest approach of all, fix-on-failure. *Make good* is when you take action to fix the consequences of the event. This might involve licking the drops off the wall and washing your clothes.

There are then, five strategies. Together they are the ART of PM, and they sum up all the possible management actions.

Figure 3.10 also illustrates another planning point. Four of the five risk strategies involve taking management action, and incur costs *before* the risk occurs. It is probably this fact, coupled with the chance of non-occurrence, which leads to so many projects, so many project managers, and so many project governance groups opting for the 'make good' strategy. It is usually by far the most expensive option should it be used, but is cost-free otherwise. I guess, in the end, it is an excellent example of how insurance is always, initially at least, a grudge purchase!

So having now discussed issues and risks from a planning perspective, what does happen when the monitoring of an assumption detects that

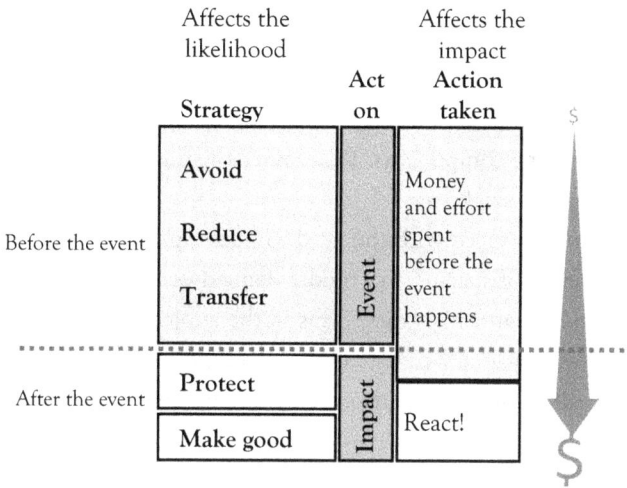

Figure 3.10 The five risk strategies

it is no longer valid? The assumption is converted into either an issue or a risk. Effectively that means identifying an owner and constructing the problem statement in such a way as to reveal what the risk or the issue is. And, most importantly, what management actions and what planning changes will be implemented to reflect this change from monitored assumption to active management. This is why understanding the set of relationships—the regulative principles that exist between worries, problems, assumptions, risks, and issues—as summed up by Figure 3.6 is important. The four linked concepts are set out in Table 3.1.

Table 3.1 From concern to risk—some definitions

A project worry Something that might happen but we have no plans to do anything about it
A project problem Something that has occurred that is within the remit of the project manager and is resolved through project management troubleshooting processes
Project issue A situation that exists, or it is known will exist, that the project manager MUST 'escalate' for resolution
Project risk A threat or hazard that MIGHT happen, and if it does will have a negative impact on the achievement of the project objectives

Reflections

This chapter focuses on developing the tactical aspects of a project plan: a series of progressive elaborations based on a step-by-step analysis of seven of the constituent components. Remember there is no *one* right way to plan, but there is a right way.

When you are faced with the need to plan a project where success is defined in terms of specific and rigidly defined constraints the sequence set out in this chapter is varied. This is the subject of *Adaptive Project Planning* (Worsley and Worsley 2019).

Considering your own experience in running projects:

1. Many WBSs combine products and tasks in the same structure. How do you ensure they don't become confused? How do you make use of this analysis when scheduling?
2. How many types of project logs do you maintain? Does your PMO maintain a centralized log of risks and issues? How do you distinguish between risks and issues?
3. Is there an argument for producing a project schedule for six or more months ahead? What situations would you see it as sensible to agree to do this with your project sponsor?
4. How do you determine whether the risk assessment of a project is adequate? Do you use lessons learned from previous projects routinely to challenge and inform the project risk log of your current project?
5. How do you ensure issues are escalated and resolved in a timely fashion?

CHAPTER 4

Portfolio Management

Planning a Portfolio

This chapter is about planning project portfolios. It might not have occurred to you that portfolios have, or even need, plans, but they do. They just aren't like project plans. In Chapter 1, we suggested that every plan has three components: its architectonic, the constituent elements, and the regulative principles. For a project, these are respectively: the strategy and structure of the project; the scope, risks, assumptions, and so on; and the project management disciplines that link them. For a portfolio, the three are the businesses' strategy, the candidate projects, and the rules used to prioritize them.

While for projects, control is exercised *within* the project, in portfolios it is the control *across* projects that must be planned for. This results in a rather different governance structure and approach. The M Model represents the governance layers that exist within a portfolio (Figure 4.1).

Notice how the decision-making around the selection of a project is taken at the portfolio governance level, not the project level. In portfolios, the decision to fund a project is made within the context of the other competing projects. We still need sponsors and clients for the project, and they motivate for its start-up, but ultimately it is the decision of the portfolio governance group as to whether the project merits a place in the portfolio.

Approvals, 'the product is good, let's do more.' occur at the project level; however, *authorization to proceed* is pushed up into the portfolio governance. If the project cannot maintain its priority, its alignment with the business strategy, or indeed if the business strategy changes, then the portfolio governance may choose to slow the project down, mothball the project, or even terminate it prematurely.

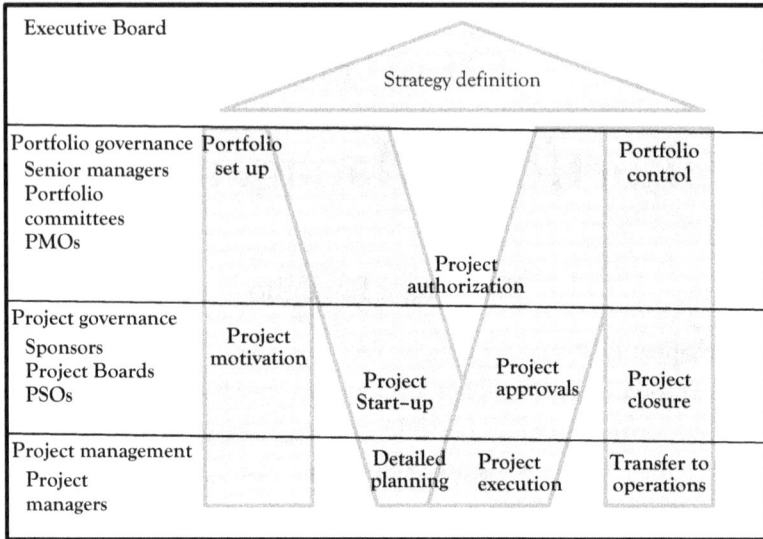

Figure 4.1 Managing the enterprise project portfolio (the M Model)

One of the features of the M Model representation is that the governance layers are not overlapping—something often overlooked in some project organizations! In an attempt to simplify and decrease the time spent in meetings, organizations mix up steering groups, sponsor meetings, and portfolio decision groups. This undermines the portfolio management process as managers become unclear as to the remit of their decision making.

The Role of the Portfolio Manager

Some portfolio managers, especially those with strong project backgrounds, interpret their role as being a multi-project manager. They see it as their responsibility to make sure that all the projects are completed satisfactorily. That just isn't so—that is the remit of each one of the project managers. Others see their role primarily as reducing conflict for resources. They do this by prioritizing and re-prioritizing access to labor and kit, leading to an endless game of juggling as each solution generates the next bottleneck.

Neither of these views is correct. The real job of project portfolio management is to maximize the throughput of projects that implement the *deliberate* strategy of the organization—and that is the continuing challenge addressed by the second planning role: portfolio control—or managing the optimum portfolio.

A story from June 8, 1944, illustrates this point well. It's the penultimate year of the world war in Europe. The Allies have landed in Normandy, and the problem is logistics—how to get enough trucks carrying supplies to the troops. Each vehicle is loaded with deliverables. A skilled individual—the driver—is in charge of each truck and has a clear objective: get the load to a specific destination by a time.

He has a plan of how to get there. His job is delivery. However, the drivers are not at liberty to just drive off the ships and get on with their job—not at all! The resulting free-for-all, as each truck competed for the limited space and resources of the quayside would have clogged up the docks and the exit routes. In its wisdom, the Army put in 'beach masters'; individuals whose job it was to shape and channel the flow of traffic to maximize throughput.

If a truck broke down, the beach masters didn't fix it, and they didn't go and mentor the driver either—they had it pushed off the road, even into the sea. Why? Because their role was to maximize the number of trucks that got through, not make sure every truck got through.

So how does this relate to modern project-based organizations? These also have skilled drivers (project managers) who are all about delivery; and these too compete for scarce resources, and by their focus on their projects, create bottlenecks. Portfolio managers (the beach masters) are there to optimize the use of resources and to de-conflict projects, specifically with the aim of maximizing throughput.

But is the problem ever that simple? When one truck is much the same as the next—all trucks are trucks—then this model works well. Just suppose, however, some trucks are more valuable than others. Is ammunition more valuable than food supplies? What about mail for the troops? Is it ever right to rescue a truck, rather than ditch it in the sea? How can the beach master know which of these tarpaulin-covered trucks, which all look the same, should be treated differently?

To solve this problem the beach master could attempt to rank the trucks—prioritize one over another. But this is a fool's errand—or requires a god's perspective. Which of the tens of possible prioritization schemes should be used? Whose value system should be imposed—and how do you deal with the fluid, changing needs of troops whose requirements are unknowable to anybody? You see some project portfolio managers struggling with similar dilemmas. They are acting as the beach masters. Some construct priority schemes, sometimes based on arcane factors, sometimes on seriously flawed business cases, and make decisions based on the rankings.

There is, however, one thing they do know for sure: someone, presumably in a position to know, thought every truck's load was sufficiently valuable to be placed on the ship. So in this scenario, the 'desirability' of each truck is decided, and the role is focused on 'do-ability,' getting as many off the ship as quickly as possible.

Change the situation slightly so that some trucks are blazoned with a 'value' indicator with some trucks ranked higher than others. Now the beach masters know which trucks (projects) are carrying the most useful/valuable deliverables. They can now give those the best chance to get through—even to the extent of siphoning off fuel or swapping parts from less valuable trucks—the equivalent of giving favored projects more resources. Of course, the truck drivers, once they realize what the special markings mean (that they wouldn't be unceremoniously abandoned or pushed into the sea), seek to get these precious markings showing value. You can see similar behaviors with projects, and it may be one reason why there are so many spurious project business cases—you may know some of them!

There remains a problem, however, that no prioritization scheme addresses—it has become a much more prevalent problem in modern times with the modularization of projects—and it caused very unusual behavior by beach masters. What is the correct marshaling behavior when a load (a significant output) is distributed between two or more trucks?

Suppose you are transporting a big gun. The barrel is in truck 1; the breech is in truck 2, and the wheels are in truck 3. What do you do if truck 1 breaks down? Ditch it in the sea, of course—worked well last time! But now there is a difference: if you ditch truck 1, you should also ditch trucks 2 and 3 as they now have no value. They are a waste of road space as wheels, and a breechblock can't deliver shells onto an enemy target!

What about if truck 3 breaks down after truck 1 and 2 have already gone? To 'rescue' the investment already made by sending the other trucks, perhaps we need a more supportive strategy to get truck 3 back in service. Now maybe we should take time and effort to mend the truck…

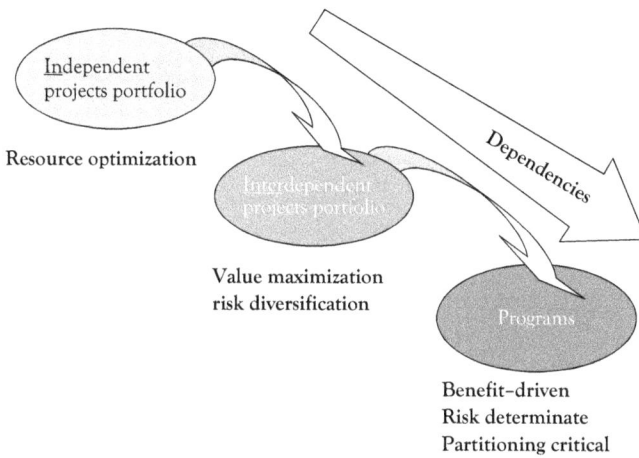

Figure 4.2 From independent project portfolio to program

In this situation, the beach master has to make much more complex decisions. How do you take the decision? What determines value now? It is this problem—the problem of value that only becomes manifest through interdependencies—that led to the creation of programs, and their management.

This progression from projects, to sets of independent projects, to linked projects, to interdependent projects shown in Figure 4.2 and the changing demands made on planning lies behind the differences between project management, portfolio management, and program management. We will come back to programs in the next chapter.

The final success of D-Day was in large part due to logistics and was all about delivery. The story of the beach masters works, in my mind, because the project management community is also about delivery. The planners in 1944 had to solve problems about getting the right stuff in the right places by the right time in complex logistical and resource-constrained environment—so do senior managers today. The Army solved their problems using trucks, manifestos, and beach masters: we solve ours by using project, portfolio, and program management disciplines, appropriately.

Challenge 1: Portfolio Setup

The D-Day story reveals how important getting the right trucks on the ship is for any management process to work effectively. So how do you

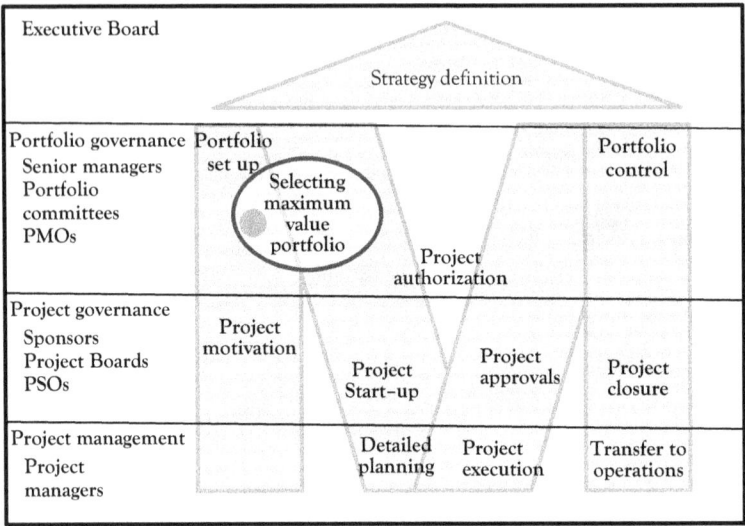

Figure 4.3 Challenge 1: Setting the maximum value portfolio

get the right trucks—selecting the 'best' combination of projects in the portfolio? (See Challenge 1 in Figure 4.3).

One approach is to apply three filters, in the right order: first, maximize value, then optimize resource use, and finally, if you need to and can, diversify risk.

Maximize Value

To maximize anything you need to be able to measure it, but what is being measured here is desirability, and that has proved to be notoriously difficult to do. There is no single agreed value system—there are many. So how do you resolve this? Any approach that ignores the self-evident fact that there are different value systems and tries to drive to a single system—reduce everything to cost—or to tries to rank them linearly is doomed. Others, like Kaplan's balanced scorecard or Parker and Benson's (1988) information economics model, are better. Rules can be published that allow different value systems to co-exist, with summing and individualized ranking accepted. Maximization can now be calculated. Perhaps even more importantly, as the composition of projects and stakeholders that are contributors to the various value systems change, the impacts can be evaluated, compared, and rational decisions made.

Optimize the Use of Resources

This filter is based on assessing do-ability. In practice, what happens is that 'optimum use' is reinterpreted as 'least idle time,' and the goal becomes the maximum utilization of the available resources rather than the most effective use of them. Why do portfolio managers do that? It is of course much easier to measure maximum use than optimum use, and that does make it attractive. The problem is that maximizing use of resources distorts the purpose of portfolios. It is a simple exercise to prove that it leads to the wrong projects being done and strategically important projects being delayed or passed over in favor of the trivial. It will inevitably lead to operational rather strategic projects being favored. A situation that frustrates so many senior managers.

It also is a significant contributor to the degradation of throughput, as portfolio managers struggle with resource conflict as part of controlling the portfolio, and increases the incidence of time slicing—that is sharing resources across projects. Provably successful when done in small amounts, time slicing, when overused, has a disastrous impact on individual productivity and thus the throughput of projects (see Figure 4.4).

The principles behind optimizing the use of resources are thoroughly analyzed by Goldratt and Cox (1984) in their 'theory of constraints'

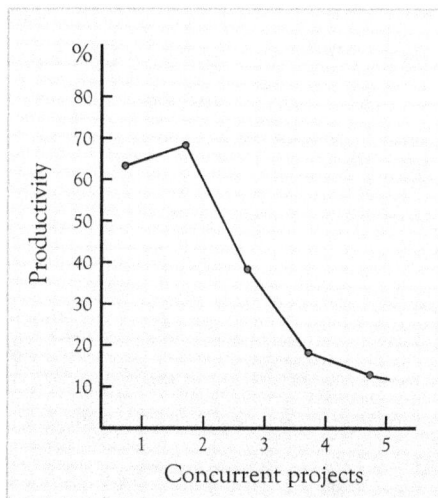

Figure 4.4 Impact on productivity of time slicing (adapted from Wheelwright and Clark 1992)

which develops the concept of scarce or 'golden' resources. When people or kit cannot be easily substituted or augmented, then throughput through them determines the overall throughput of the system. They are easy to recognize because work tasks pile up waiting for their availability and attention.

To maximize throughput, planning and management attention needs to be paid to the rate of delivery of work to these resources. The scarce resources should be planned for 100 percent utilization. Any task that can be done by any other means should be done by an alternative, and any backlog should be managed down. A good solution for projects is often to recognize scarce resources and manage them as assets rather than as resources. The scare resource time is diarized—treating their allocation to tasks as a series of appointments—rather than calendared where the project manager allocates work in what is otherwise a block of unstructured time.

Optimizing Resources in a Retail Portfolio

Customer relationship management systems, such as SAP CRM are the life-blood of retail organizations today. One of the consequences of this is that retail organizations are increasingly dependent upon their CRM systems and in turn, they are dependent upon the IT suppliers and the resources that have the skills to develop and maintain these systems. Projects and programs which utilize CRM are competing for limited—even scarce—resources, not just internally, but against other large consumers of similar resources across the retail sector. We interviewed a portfolio manager at a leading SA-based grocery retailer on how she deals with these issues.

> Having insufficient specialists really affects our projects and creates elapsed time delays which our business customers don't understand—they don't realize why we have the problem. Within a year, the costs of these constrained resources can increase by over 20 percent. This makes budgeting and forecasting future spend much more difficult. We have ways of dealing with this, but business is not interested—they just want what they want.

When the resource constraint is triggered by competition: competing both internally and externally for access to the resource, the planning process needs to adopt a different strategy from that of determining clearance rates.

The first approach is to treat the scarce resource as an asset and then to rearrange the sequence of tasks to make use of the availability of their specific skills. Keeping these resources effective is much more important than worrying about overall efficiency. This may do violence to the standard scheduling processes, but that is a small price to pay in comparison to using less skilled people on specialist tasks.

The second approach used to good effect is to anticipate and hire specialist contractors ahead of need—jump the gun so as to speak—and induct them into the environment and system before the project is launched. The advantage is that this reduces, by up to three months, the lead-time before which they are not fully productive. It does, however, raise cost issues. From some perspectives, this is 'idle time;' and introduces potential HR issues: keeping people hanging on while decisions are made about whether the project will go ahead is not easy. It can lead to wasted recruitment effort and may risk the goodwill of the contractors.

The portfolio manager maintains a close watch on the resources that limit the throughput on her projects. Resource capacity management in portfolios is notoriously difficult to do, but less so if you focus your monitoring effort specifically on those critical resources that you know will be the bottleneck.

All project proposals are analyzed for the call they make on critical resources. If an acceptable plan can be constructed that avoids the use of these resources, then this is the first route. If not, then the project is prioritized, using resource-first scheduling techniques, against all the other projects in the portfolio making demands on the same critical resource. This approach leads neatly to the third filter.

Diversify Sources of Risk

When you've ranked all the projects within the value systems of the organization (desirability) and moderated that list by taking resource availability and conflicts into account (do-ability), there may still be options, different combinations of projects that fall within the envelope. If there are—if you have the luxury of choice—the final decider lies in reducing as far as possible the level of risk exposure. This means ensuring the portfolio is not unduly open to failure from a single source of risk—over dependence on a single approach, a single supplier, or a single technology.

By applying these three filters in this stepwise approach, the organization now has the best portfolio it can have to deliver its corporate strategy. This is what sits behind the portfolio selection technique called the 'efficient frontier.'

The *efficient frontier* is a technique for optimizing the selection of projects in a project portfolio.

See Figure 4.5. The dimensions of 'risk-adjusted value' and 'risk-adjusted cost' take into account the level of uncertainty in the estimates of benefits and the costs. A practical alternative surrogate measure for risk-adjusted costs is to use the amount of scarce resource each project requires.

All possible combinations of projects—defined in terms of their value and cost—are considered, leading to the creation of thousands of possible portfolios. Portfolios having just one project, portfolios with every possible pair of projects, and so on. These are then charted against total portfolio value and total portfolio cost.

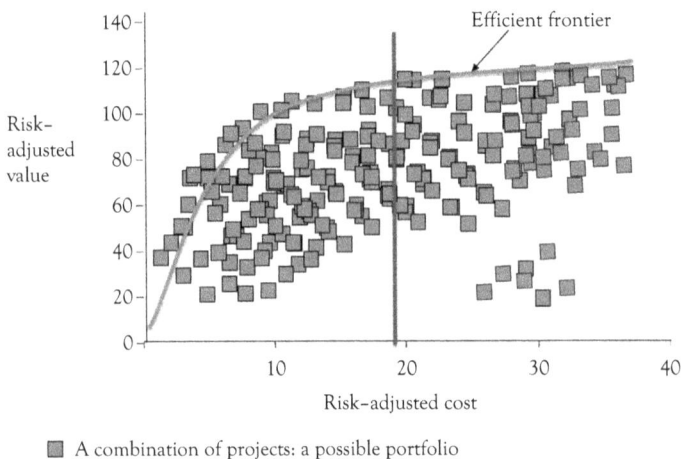

■ A combination of projects: a possible portfolio

Figure 4.5 The efficient frontier

Dropping the budget line identifies all the portfolios that can be afforded. Those potential portfolios that cluster around the budget line near the efficient frontier line are those that represent the best return for the investment. The final choice between the candidate portfolios can now be informed by paying regard to the types of risk and selecting the portfolio where these are most diversified.

Challenge 2: Portfolio Control

There remains a problem though. No matter how well the initial portfolio planning was carried out, things change. Business priorities change, and therefore the relative desirability of projects in the portfolio and candidate projects change too, and new opportunities and threats emerge. So how do you plan appropriately in this circumstance?

What the M Model illustrates (see Figure 4.6) are the two management demands made on portfolio managers: one is establishing the portfolio, and the other is controlling it. Control involves changing the projects under management in the in-flight portfolio.

With throughput being the condition of success for project portfolio management, then most decision making will involve re-assigning assets

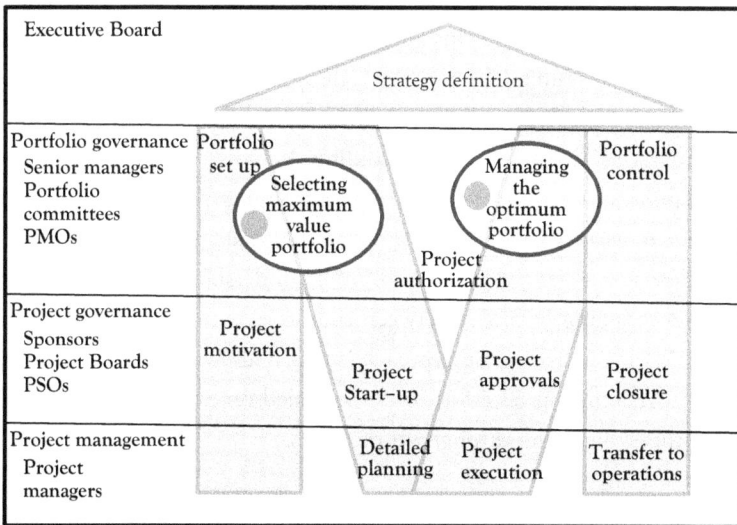

Figure 4.6 Challenge 2: Managing the optimum portfolio

and resources to eliminate bottlenecks, introducing different processes to reduce time delays caused by bottlenecks, and re-structuring the phasing of projects to avoid bottlenecks.

Whichever way you look at it, in the end, the portfolio manager has to handle the consequences of a high and fluctuating demand for resource and limited and relatively static capacity. The three options are:

1. Collect total resource demands for each project and establish a demand forecast. Sounds like a possible solution but in practice, it does not work. It generates far too much information and requires an unrealistic level of accuracy, certainly well beyond the management reach of most project managers. The process becomes unwieldy, and planning is too unresponsive.

2. Only consider scarce resources and model those—perhaps treating them as assets rather than as resources. This has the merit of significantly decreasing the volume of data needed to be collected and focuses attention on the primary sources of bottlenecks. It is highly sensitive to making the correct choices about exactly what and who is a critical resource, and demands a discipline within projects that is not always there: that projects use the resources in line with the schedule—an ambition not satisfied by many projects.

3. The third option is much more dynamic than the first two. Called 'balanced resourcing,' this approach also focuses on the deployment of scarce resources. It, however, relies on short-term resource forecasting, with five to 10 working day horizons, obviating the problems associated with poor scheduling. It allows the project office to respond quickly and responsively to changing project situations. It, too, makes its own demands on project managers and the project office as it relies on a clear and public understanding of the relative and changing priorities between the projects in the portfolio. One major advantage of the approach is that it allows much higher levels of work-in-progress effort to be expended on non-strategic projects without incurring throughput penalties.

One organization that uses the third option recounts a lovely story that underpins the need for a shared sense of corporate citizenship when running an enterprise-level portfolio. The portfolio manager realized it was all working as it should when a senior manager stood up and said to a colleague in a governance meeting, "I recognize that your project is more important to the company [than mine], your project should get the resource."

Of course, the commonest approach is to introduce time slicing, where a resource is considered to be infinitely divisible and can be shared across projects. We've touched upon its attractiveness and the downsides, and the inevitability of severe resource conflict in a regime in which project portfolios are planned to have maximum resource utilization from the start. So we now need to discuss culling.

Challenge 3: Culling Projects

Project culling is the third portfolio management challenge, (see Figure 4.7.) It is an essential process in planning a portfolio. Stopping projects, which are addressing yesterday's problems, is probably even more important than starting projects designed to address today's, but in our experience, it is rarely used.

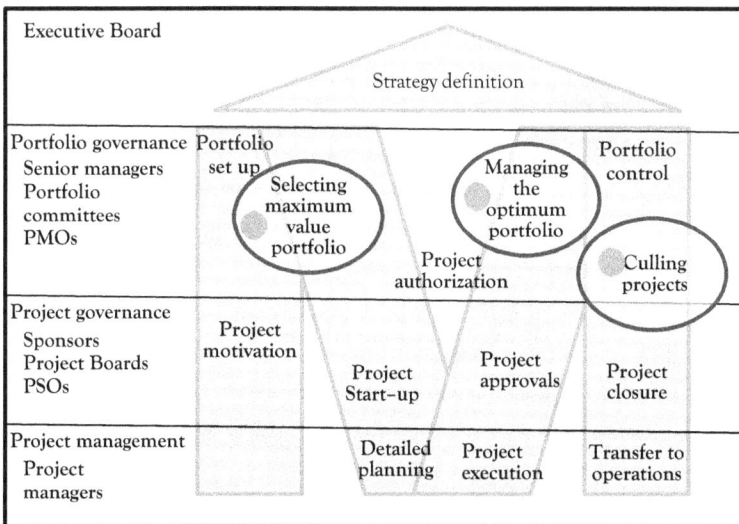

Figure 4.7 Challenge 3: Culling projects

Even though many organizations are running more projects that they can resource, and where planned resources are no longer available due to organizational retrenchment, the response is often more of a starvation process than a strategic exercise. Resources and budgets are cut 'across the board' and in the scramble of re-scheduling projects; survival often depends upon the level of senior management commitment and political 'clout.' This in itself is not a bad thing. Projects with top management support are consistently shown to perform better. However, it does undermine strategic portfolio planning principles.

Deliberate culling, on the other hand, is a principled elimination of those projects, which do not now meet the desirability and do-ability characteristics required to keep them in the 'portfolio pack.'

Culling is the process of reducing an animal population that has overtaken the natural resources available for its continued healthy continuation. The process—as horrific as it can be to observe—is sometimes necessary. The standard practice is to target sick, old, and redundant individuals, leaving a healthier and viable population. Precisely the same principles should be applied to culling projects. Target projects for culling are firstly those whose desirability is low, or at least lower than others, and secondly where their do-ability depends on access to scarce resources which is out of proportion to their worth.

Even in the case where initiation and planning authorization processes were carried out well, previous cut-off levels may no longer be stringent enough in the new, more constrained environment. Such factors do not remain stable over the life of a portfolio, and projects with long execution stages may not have been reassessed, in some cases, for years. In a 2011 review of 15 client portfolios, it was reported that during the annual portfolio prioritization more than one-third of the projects and programs approved were carried forward from previous years, with 20 percent having survived two annual review processes. The question perhaps to ask is—does this reflect a real need for long-term projects or is it that management decision making around stopping something is just so much harder than approving a project to start?

If you are considering stopping a project in the execution stage, you do have to take into account, 'stoppability.' In a recent analysis of three large portfolios, which had undergone a torrid cutback exercise, we found that projects just don't go away that easily:

- Well over 30 percent of supposedly curtailed project activities were continuing below the portfolio radar. In these cases, the project office was reporting the projects as terminated, while effort, directly trackable back to the project, was still being applied.
- All three of the portfolios were misaligned against the strategically-agreed balanced scorecard, with one portfolio now having 80 percent of its active projects in the 'business-as-usual' category with just one project in the category of business development.
- Not one project had been *officially* terminated—they appeared to be 'dying on the vine.'

Any project which is past initiation will be accelerating—engaging resources and stakeholder attention. To terminate early means the project activities have to be stepped down in a controlled fashion; else the collateral damage may cause degradation in unexpected ways and places. The problem is exacerbated when the project is within a portfolio. Resources, outputs, and impacts on the business maybe interlinked and the consequences of any action taken unclear.

While this fear, uncertainty, and doubt are likely to cause a delay of itself, it also contributes to the psychological pressure on the project team to 'just finish this' before stopping.

There are at least two forces at work: the first is inertia—change is more troublesome than steady state, the second is more subtle and caught so aptly by Magnus Magnusson (the original host of Mastermind) in his bye line "I've started, so I'll finish…"

This phenomenon is well documented in the field of organizational and human decision making as a concept known as the 'escalation of commitment.' Even in the face of obvious and clear negative consequences, decision makers will maintain or increase resource commitment and risk further losses.

Originally analyzed as the impact of sunk costs on decision making, it has strong resonance in project-based management actions and is often regarded as political commonsense that once you have spent a lot of money you really shouldn't give up.

"To terminate a project in which $1.1 billion has been invested represents an unconscionable mishandling of taxpayers' dollars" (Senator Denton 1984).

The feeling that we have invested too much to quit is psychologically compelling but is irrational. There are myriad examples of projects, especially government ones, where, in the face of diminishing returns, the economically rational decision has been overturned by the desire (unsupported by any historical evidence) to recover something from the investment.

In recent years, research has found that project participants were unduly affected, not by sunk costs, but by the project's closeness to completion. In fact, when the project is close to being finished, project participants often recommend completing the project even when it is clearly economically unwise to do so. The escalation of commitment explains why project activities continue even when the project has been 'terminated.' It manifests itself by enlisting senior commitment to undermine the termination order; slowness in actioning close-out activities; the continuation of project activities in secret; or simply blatant continuation of the project activity in the belief that the problem will go away or be moved to somebody else's project.

The Challenges of Stopping a Project

The project closeout stage is generally estimated at around 3 to 7 percent of the total expenditure on a project. Apart from exhortations to do it, and to do it properly, there is little valuable guidance on what's important at this stage. Even PRINCE2®, a market leader in project methodologies, merely states that "Every project should come to a controlled close," and lists nine administrative activities, none of which address the fundamental purpose of a closeout.

Discussions of project closeout usually focus on the organizational benefits from managing lessons learned and the fundamental need to transfer capability into the operational environment. The literature largely ignores the necessity of ensuring that the outputs from the project are handed over to their new owners in such a way that at least some of the desired beneficial outcomes occur, or of ensuring that the stakeholders and team members are debriefed, both technically and emotionally.

These last two goals are even more important on a project that has been terminated early. The pressure to walk away as early as possible, to disassociate from what will be perceived as a 'failed' project, and the desire to become engaged in something valued, all work toward abbreviating the closeout process following culling.

In fact, there is a clear case that early termination leads to a need for an extended closeout process to support the salvaging of residual value from the project. As reported by one project manager:

> *The project was stopped after six months. While it had another three months scheduled to run, both the sponsor and I felt that what had been delivered to-date was good enough. But we had to persuade the key stakeholders of this. They just took the fact that the project had been stopped as an indication that the project had failed and therefore the outputs were of no use. Despite developing a communication plan and spending considerable time and effort in discussing the issue, it took a further month of hard communication work to get them signed up to using the new and entirely effective processes.*

Getting the Return from Early Project Termination

Stopping a project badly is a 'double whammy' hit on portfolio performance. Not only are the planned project benefits lost or reduced, but also the cost savings anticipated from the termination are not fully realized.

The challenge is to ensure that project culling is systematically and beneficially applied. The culling process must maintain the linkage to normal portfolio decision making while taking into account the 'termination risks,' that is the risks associated with stopping the project and realizing the return from stopping the project. The questions to be asked are: Can we be successful in turning off the effort and expenditure being applied to the project? If the culling is to reduce costs; can any of the CAPEX costs be avoided? If the focus is on the release of resources; how quickly and effectively will these resources be redeployed?

Without a process for determining and following through the termination of projects, project culling becomes a subjective, political and tactical process which encourages 'dog eat dog' behaviors between project staff and undermines any attempts to implement strategic portfolio monitoring and control.

The need to terminate projects within a portfolio is not a transient problem brought on us by the need to retrench. It is a natural consequence of running portfolios with changing and competing priorities. The culling processes should be an integral part of the portfolio management process with clear and understood accountabilities built into the portfolio management structure. Closing out a project crucially must involve the management of the close down of the commitment levels of all the stakeholders. Without this, the project is likely to suffer a prolonged, ineffective, and potentially costly death—most likely as not to be reborn out of the ashes at some later date.

Reflections

Portfolios are not examples of multi-project management, where project managers time-slice their day, spending time on different projects. Some project roles demand exactly that, but that is not portfolio management. While for projects, control is exercised *within* the project, in portfolios it is the control *across* projects that must be planned for. This results in a rather different governance structure and approach which is represented by the M Model. It means that the processes of portfolio management focus on the appropriate prioritization, review, and control and culling of projects.

Consider these questions:

1. If you are project managing several projects concurrently, how do you resolve the conflict of interests between the prioritization demands made by the competing projects?

2. When a project is to be terminated, how and when do you engage with the stakeholders involved?

3. When additional projects are introduced into the in-flight portfolio, how are the additional resource and management demands accommodated?

4. How are conflicts between the sponsors and stakeholders for a project and the demands of the portfolio resolved when the same individuals are on both committees (project board and portfolio board)?

5. What criteria are used to place projects on your roadmap and how is the composition of your portfolio finally decided? How useful are your business cases? Is any use made of a 'balanced' portfolio concept? If so, how is it used?

CHAPTER 5

Planning a Program

What's Different About a Program?

Programs differ from projects and portfolios in that their purpose is about the delivery of a vision, not just value, and definitely not just outputs. This changes everything. The role of the program manager is to establish a coordinated, co-operating set of capabilities and ensure these do deliver a transformed organization. So, planning a program is not project planning writ large. The skills are different, the tools are different, and the thinking is different.

The architectonic of a program—the way a program is structured to deliver its vision—is composed of workstreams, tranches, and transition states (possibly unfamiliar words right now, but not for long). The constituent elements are the projects and line-based work tasks. The regulative principles are the interdependencies and interoperability conditions that exist between the impacts, the products, the resources, and the timing decisions that ultimately determine the management of the program.

Ultimately, project managers are interested in the outputs of their project, the physical things delivered. The sum of them is the project's scope and a critical tactical concern for the project manager is that the scope is controlled. Many a project has been subject to the scourge of project managers—scope creep.

For program managers it is different. Their delivery is the vision, and their concern is not the physical vehicles used to deliver it. In principle, they are agnostic or should be, as to what the projects physically deliver, as long as the impacts and outcomes are acceptable. Their focus, as we will see later in this chapter, is the program boundary, not its scope.

The following story illustrates why this is so important. The program is one that many organizations that are going 'digital' have had to run, and are usually called 'IAM' programs, standing for 'Identity and Access Mechanisms.' The vision for this program was:

The PMI (2017) list five process groups: Initiating, Planning, Executing, Monitoring and Control, and Closing, and suggest that project managers need to understand how these are integrated to deliver the project management process.

For programs, we have found it useful to organize program management disciplines in to these four:

- *Stakeholder management*: Facilitating, brokering, communicating, and championing change
- *Strategy management*: Optioneering, constraint management, structuring, and planning
- *Resource management*: resource strategy, sourcing, and developing capability
- *Delivery management*: Monitoring, controlling, and integrating

NewCo recognizes me* as having a unique identity with my own personal level of privileges and accesses. NewCo knows my history and provides me with relevant and appropriate access to allow me to conduct the transactions expected of me.

*me is either a person, a set of devices or a systems entity

Notice the vision does not say how this will be achieved, just that it will. The program had four workstreams, one of which was to implement a customized 'off-the-shelf' product sold by a large software house. After months of effort, it could not be made to work. Had this been a project, or a badly structured program, it would mean failure. As it was, there was no commitment to this solution, or any solution, just to the outcome, which was handily achieved using an entirely different suite of capabilities.

A Program Life Cycle

Unlike projects, programs don't have formalized life cycles, but we have found the sequence shown in Figure 5.1 useful when helping firms set up programs for the first time.

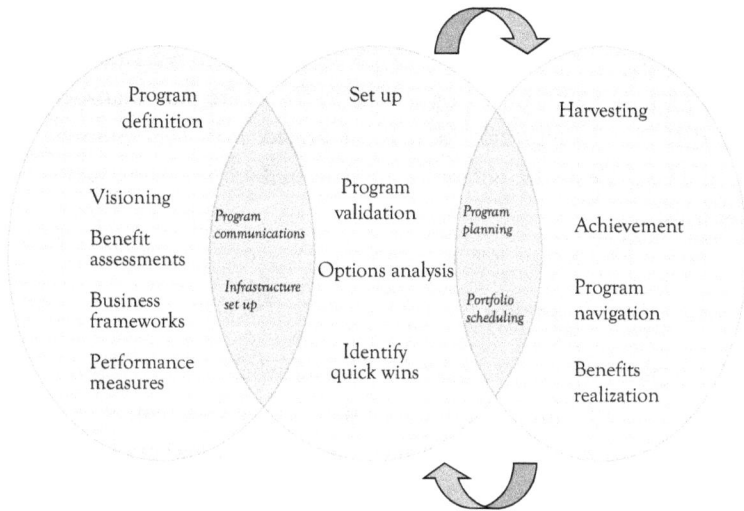

Figure 5.1 A program life cycle

Program definition can take between six weeks and 18 months. The outputs from this, often intense period, is a compelling view of the future state to be achieved, which is supported by a set of strategic and financial benefits. And to make sure the vision is not just a dream, there needs to be, at least in outline, a target operating model or blueprint of the infrastructure that will maintain the vision, together with key performance indicators or performance measures.

Sometimes the 'ask' is too much, and nothing substantive ever emerges, as the key stakeholders cannot agree on a coherent vision and the program is stillborn. A far worse situation prevails when there is a 'dash to the cash,' with a program initiated with no agreement and no commitment. In this circumstance, the set up stage never comes together and the program stalls, with recriminations and a feeling that programs are far too hard.

Moving out of the first stage in to 'Set up' for the first time, the program emerges from its cloistered beginnings and is exposed to a much wider audience. Program validation occurs as the various involved parties jockey for position and the vision becomes grounded, taking into account additional perspectives. Opportunities to develop momentum are sought and ways to deliver the vision and blueprint tested, and forms the basis for the first tranche of work.

The iteration between Set up and Harvesting is a distinctive feature of programs and is the basis for the use of tranches shown in Figure 5.2. It reinforces the observation made already that a program manager's role is to deliver outcomes, not, as it is for project managers, outputs, and also unlike projects the outcomes are delivered within the program, not after it.

Planning with Tranches

Program planning sets out what to do, and when to do it, by deciding how best to combine projects and other managed activities to deliver value to the organization at regular intervals—at the end of each tranche. The end of each tranche is identified as a 'transition state.' Thus, programs are planned in time-boxes, with an end-state that leaves the organization in a valued and relatively stable state.

> A *tranche* is a group of projects and line activities in a program that will deliver the planned impacts, outcomes, capabilities and benefits.

A good touchstone when considering whether or not a tranche is well-defined is to check that the organization could successfully continue in this new transition state for a reasonable period of time, possibly indefinitely in the case that the program does not proceed. This is a stringent condition and one that a fair few numbers of programs we have reviewed fail to achieve.

As shown in Figure 5.2, a program is composed of a number of tranches. The future state—or the 'to be' state—is a physical instance of the target operating model of the transformed organization. (Program management has had to create new words and new meanings of words to prevent the essential ideas being muddled with project terms.)

A tranche is composed of a number of projects (and line activities). Some of the component projects are for research, and their only purpose is to establish the feasibility of an approach. (The 'R' in the boxes in Figure 5.2 represent this.) Such projects are strictly time-boxed and budget-constrained. Enablers—the 'E' projects—are projects that don't deliver any value but which are necessary building blocks that make the

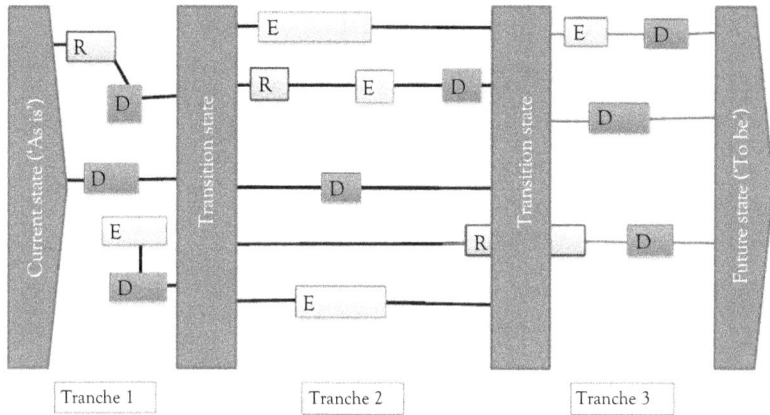

Figure 5.2 A program

delivery of benefits from projects identified with a 'D,' more manageable, and sometimes even possible, to achieve.

Selecting Projects in a Tranche

When program managers, or indeed organizations, new to programs, create their initial program structures, it is quite common to see them end up with a version of a multi-phased project. In such a case, you see the first tranche loaded with feasibility studies, together with a few enablers. The second tranche is mainly filled with more enabling projects, and the third tranche, if ever the program is allowed to get that far, is intended to have the delivery of the valuable stuff.

This approach fails on so many levels. First, it pays virtually no attention to the needs and expectations of the stakeholders. It ignores one of the main purposes of programs, which is the early delivery of sustainable value—particularly in environments where in order to achieve the vision there needs to be a collaboration of change initiatives. When you see such program structures, it is clear that the planning is driven by internal project dynamics rather than the demand for incremental organizational change. To achieve significant or transformational change often requires a program to be responsive to, to build on the energy, and adapt to the unintended consequences of those changes it unwittingly causes.

Programs as Deliverers of Change

We have been involved with initiating, planning, and executing programs for over 20 years, and they haven't gotten any easier. One of the reasons is that transformation programs require the integration of nine different management disciplines. We developed The Change Diamond™ (see Figure 5.3) to understand how these interacted and where the boundaries lay between them.

In the model, time runs from top to bottom. The left-hand side represents the value disciplines; adoption of change and the achievement of benefits. On the right are the delivery disciplines: project management and implementation. The model has three layers that represent the three fundamental stages of any planned or directed change (as opposed to spontaneous or evolutionary change). The nine management disciplines are identified on the diamond, and the role of each is described as follows.

Make It Wanted

To develop the commitment necessary for sustained, planned change involves three management disciplines. The problem needs to be understood, and opportunities and goals identified—it demands strategic

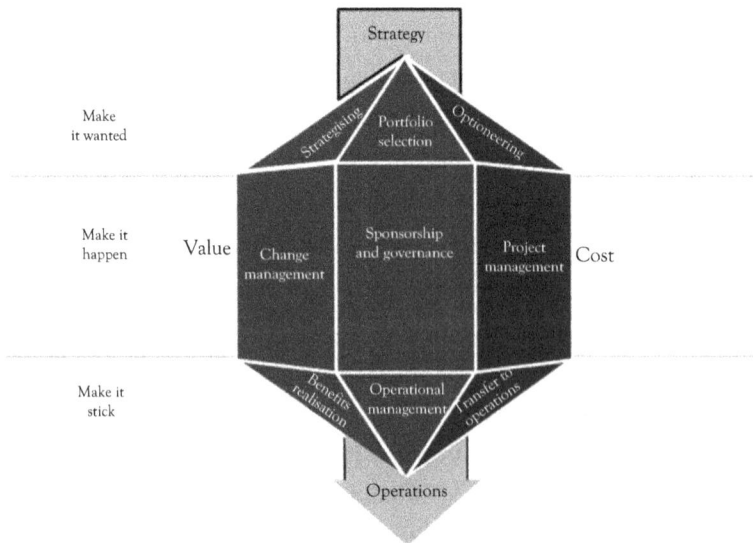

Figure 5.3 The Change Diamond™

planning or strategizing. Once confident that there really is a problem or opportunity to address, solutions can be proposed, and the risks associated with implementing them set out—optioneering. And finally, choices and decisions about which capabilities should be developed and in what sequence, and how resources will be expended leads to use of portfolio management disciplines.

Once a compelling story—the vision—has been developed and a business case established, the program brief has been agreed. The next stage is execution.

Make It Happen

The core of this layer is the sponsorship and governance disciplines for both delivery and adoption. Project management takes the lion's share of the delivery, though many line interactions are involved. Change management in all of its different manifestations: structured tasks led by change managers, behavioral and attitudinal interventions shaped by change leaders and change agents, and training all take place. The captaincy—who controls the pace and the sequence—alternates between delivery and adoption, often quite rapidly. It is the principal role of the sponsors or program directorate to ensure that this does happen, and that adoption does not get overwhelmed by the diktat of delivery.

Any loss of sponsorship commitment, any disengagement, and lack of clarity during this stage is deadly and saps the vitality from the third and in many ways the most crucial stage.

Make It Stick

The only point of all the work done and effort expended is to exploit the changed capabilities made possible through the program. This means the organization has to adopt and adapt its people, processes, and practices so that by working in the new target operating system it can deliver the vision. To effect that, outputs need to be transferred from the development environment of projects into operations; attitudes and behaviors need to become embedded so that they are the 'way things are done around here'; and the value and benefits from the new capabilities must be captured.

This is where many projects fail. Programs, due to their structure and governance, are better suited to managing this transformation and deliver a sustained future state, but it remains hard to do, and there is little support on how to do it in the literature.

Making Program Management Work

Working with a number of successful program managers, and discussing with them their experiences it seems you can boil down the really difficult challenges to:

1. Getting the structure of a program right
2. Translating a vision into everyday physical actions
3. Getting from management targets to stakeholder commitment
4. Balancing the demands of design, delivery, and change
5. On-boarding change teams
6. Delivering projects in a program—managing a tranche
   (a) Selecting the 'best' tranche
   (b) Dealing with interdependencies
   (c) Culling projects

By locating these challenges on the Change Diamond™ (see Figure 5.4) the management disciplines that get involved in dealing with them are indicated.

We consider each challenge and how to address them in the following sections.

Program Management: Challenge 1: Getting the Structure of a Program Right

The impact on the conduct of the program of not addressing Challenge 1, 'Getting the structure right' is severe. The purpose of the structuring is to deliver the vision of the program, and it can't be said often enough or loud enough, "No vision? No program." Even with a compelling vision, the problem remains how to best organize the work and the organization to transition to the new way.

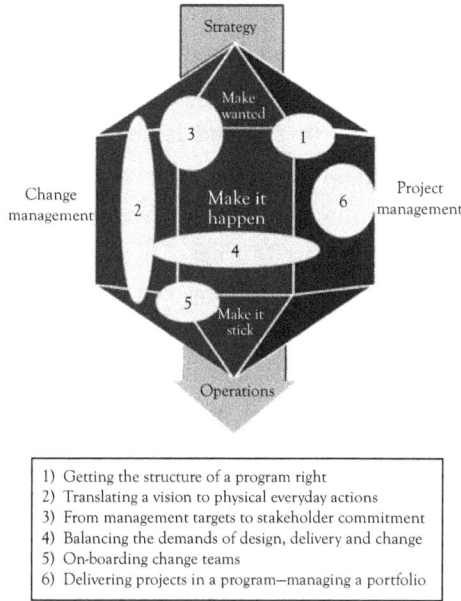

> 1) Getting the structure of a program right
> 2) Translating a vision to physical everyday actions
> 3) From management targets to stakeholder commitment
> 4) Balancing the demands of design, delivery and change
> 5) On-boarding change teams
> 6) Delivering projects in a program—managing a portfolio

Figure 5.4 The challenges of running a program

Tranches: Stepping Stones to Success

Much practical knowledge and some theoretical analysis have shown that the ideal length of a tranche within a program is between four and 11 months, with a target of around seven months. Less than four months creates too much complication. Longer than 11 months leads back to the problems that led to the creation of programs in the first place: the need to shorten delivery time to reduce the impact of changes in the organization or the marketplace on the value of the outcomes.

Given that the planning environment of a program is defined by this time-structured architectonic, it should be no surprise that projects within a tranche are often constructed differently from 'independent' projects and is one of the reasons why the governance surrounding projects within programs is different.

For instance, many of the projects in a program would not bear an independent business case. Neither would they benefit from having a sponsor in the same way as independent projects do. Being within a program means that the project's purpose is defined by the program. Their structure will often depend upon other projects that are running within the tranche, or at least within the program, and the value and even the delivery of their products will often be affected by decisions made in other projects.

One criterion that has been found to be particularly useful when deciding whether a program is well structured or not is to assess the types and numbers of project interdependencies or program critical interfaces (PCIs) that exist. The number can never be zero because if it was, it would mean the collection of projects was an independent portfolio not a program (see Figure 4.2). On the other hand, careless design can create numerous and unnecessary PCIs, and this is a problem. In a study we carried out, we found PCIs cost on average 200 person-hours of senior management time to resolve, as the issues that are thrown up are often complex, and extremely complicated to manage.

A program being run in a large retail organization to transform it from a 16/6 to a 24/7 operation, when analyzed against this criteria, had 51 interdependencies within just one of the tranches. The program had—not surprisingly—stalled. A review, followed by a restructuring of the projects within the tranche, led to the reduction of the PCIs to 11. This was achieved by aggregating and then segregating the products and tasks between the component projects so that the crucial impacts were delivered from one or two projects rather than from four to eight. Although the resourcing of the projects was now more complicated, in that resources from several parts of the organization worked together in a single project team, the management of the program was greatly simplified. As it is the delivery and management of impacts that ultimately determine whether a program is successful, this was a sensible and very effective redesign.

There are a number of other pragmatically-derived considerations when structuring a program. Other than keeping the number of PCIs down to as low a number as possible, the number of component projects is important. Having only one, two, or three projects in a tranche is likely to reflect that the program is probably just a convenient envelope for running independent projects. Having 73 projects in a tranche, which we found in one organization that was attempting to change its chart of accounts across its global subsidiaries, is far too many, and the program proved to be completely unmanageable.

So, finally, two numbers. Of the 154 programs we have been involved with, when the number of projects in a tranche rose above 22, it always led to trouble, with 11 being found to be the mode value for successful planning and successful programs.

Program Management: Challenge 2: Translating a Vision

The second challenge of 'Translating a vision into everyday physical actions' arises from the need to focus on outcomes, not on the physical basis of the solution. The best way to effect this change in thinking and planning is to start from the vision and work toward the outputs. The model shown in Figure 5.5 supports this approach.

Start from the End

The vision of the future state, as seen from the customers' point of view, is the starting point. As this is the customers' value proposition (CVP) and is a description of what is desirable from their perspective, it should be in the customers' 'voice.'

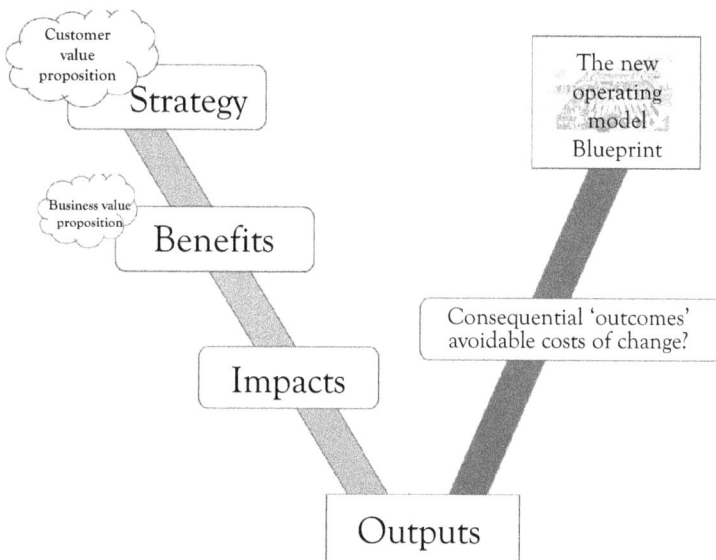

Figure 5.5 The program V model

The next step is to identify why and in what ways this set of organizational capabilities (the vision of the future) is valuable to the business. This is where traditional project benefits, the business value proposition (BVP), are set out. (Benefits are discussed in Chapter 2.)

With good stakeholder acceptance of the CVP *and* the BVP, there is some likelihood of success for the program. Unless there is both, the chances are poor.

Next, you need to identify what differences from the current state are necessary to deliver the business and customer value propositions, and how can those changes (impacts) be brought about? What project outputs, and what tasks carried out by operational management are required?

Having come down the left side of the 'V,' you have established a series of links from the benefits through a series of impacts to the products that will cause them. This is the basis of a BIP map (benefits-impacts-products) and is used to validate all further program planning. An example of a BIP map is shown in Figure 5.6. You read it from left to right, and its purpose is to identify the products and impacts and establish the management actions necessary to translate the outputs into the desired outcomes.

Having got a set of outputs, and before structuring them into projects, operational tasks and tranches, there is a further step to take. You

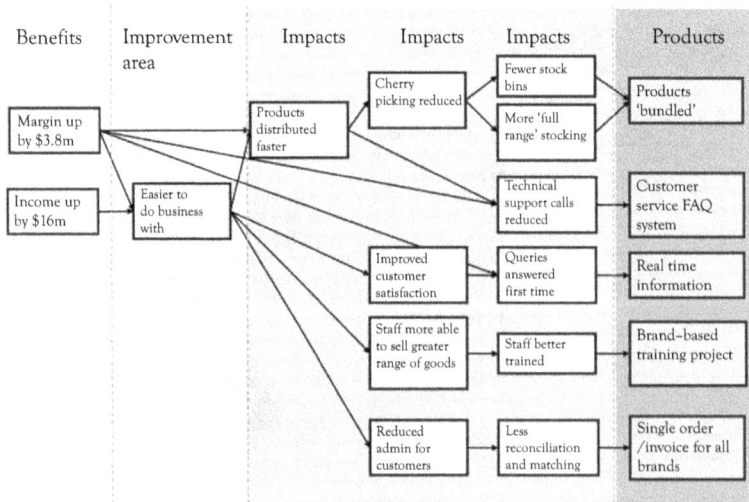

Figure 5.6 A BIP map

need to establish what operational consequences will be triggered by these suggested changes: new processes, new techniques, and possibly new staff and staffing structures. Some have adverse effects, or dis-benefits, giving rise to additional costs and other impacts, which may be unacceptable to the management team and staff. This should force a rethink. In what different ways could the value propositions be caused? This process of going up and down the arms of the V model is repeated until a solution satisfactory to all the key stakeholders is reached.

Ultimately, the set of operational impacts and consequences, in aggregate, form the new target operating model, or blueprint, of the new organization. In this way, the vision of the new world is translated into the physical reality of projects, operational changes, and a new way of working.

Causing Real Change

Figure 5.7 illustrates how a program works to deliver its vision. Firstly, governance gates connect the three stages of the program life cycle: Program Definition, Setup, and Harvesting. Their purpose is to ensure that the vision is maintained. Secondly, the program does not end with the completion of the tranches of projects, but when sufficient embedding of the new capabilities—the vision—has been achieved. And thirdly, and importantly, that programs are composed of a mixture of different types of projects and operational activities. It is one of the more commonly overlooked and underused aspects of a program manager's role, that of sponsoring and monitoring operational or line activities. Programs are not just collections of projects. To succeed they need to involve and engage with operational managers as they adopt and adapt working practices to deliver the program's vision.

Program Management: Challenge 3: From Management Targets to Stakeholder Commitment

The challenge of creating and maintaining stakeholder commitment is considerable. Programs are always stakeholder-intensive, and the sheer number of agenda-based stakeholders (Worsley 2016) is one of the most

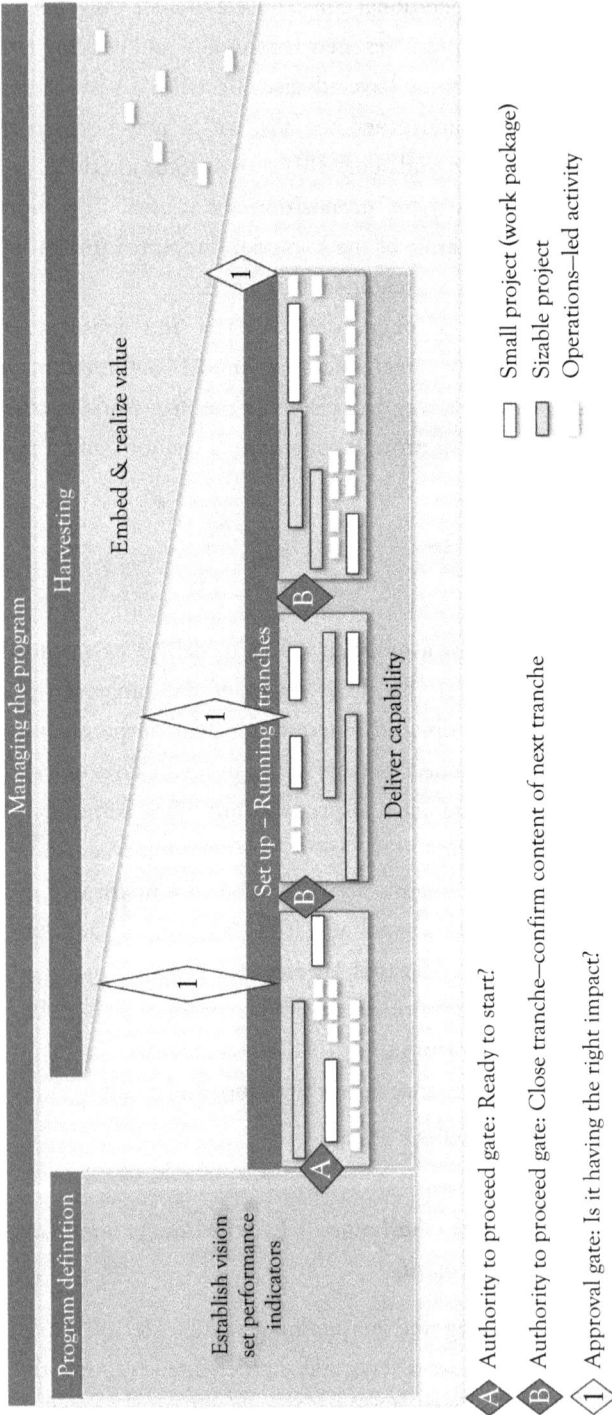

A   Authority to proceed gate: Ready to start?

B   Authority to proceed gate: Close tranche—confirm content of next tranche

1   Approval gate: Is it having the right impact?

Figure 5.7 Translating the vision into activities

time-consuming aspects of the program manager's role. But, done poorly, or not at all, is a sure path to a failed program.

Agenda-based stakeholders are those who have an opinion on and perhaps are passionate about a project and its conduct.

Role-based stakeholders are those who have a specific and identified responsibility for the conduct of a project, for example the sponsor or a steering group member.

While the *management* of role-based stakeholders may be appropriate in some circumstances, you can only *engage* with agenda-based stakeholders.

The impact of this need for commitment is so pervasive it is responsible for another difference in the planning and conduct between programs and projects, and it is a game-changer.

Boundary Management

One powerful metaphor for most programs is that they are boundary-spanning management structures, and the management of boundaries and the issues that this raises can be considered the proper remit of most program managers.

Figure 5.8 illustrates the common boundary management situations that may be found in programs. Programs cannot exist without a few committed stakeholders that share a common vision. So, you can consider illustration 1 in Figure 5.8[1] as the 'baseline' state. The boundary encompasses these committed stakeholders.

But programs also need political support. Indeed they are far more dependent upon this than most projects. The astute program manager will adapt their program to include and create supporters—essentially changing the boundaries within which the program operates (Figure 5.8[2]). How does that work in practice? It may involve including existing projects into the program with the sole intention of attracting political support. In stakeholder-intensive programs, it may entail creating new parallel projects within the program boundaries.

Parallel projects—projects that don't directly address the overall goals of a program but are necessary to ensure that stakeholders commit to, or at least don't sabotage, the program outcomes. (Worsley 2016)

It's not that the aim is to bring everybody inside the program boundary either. The program also needs allies on the outside (Figure 5.8[3]). Ask any politician; the most useful allies are those who independently endorse you. If you know someone is 'in the tent,' their support is discounted, 'of course, they'd say that wouldn't they?' It's about the judicious and sensitive positioning of the boundaries.

Getting momentum for any change can be hard, and the last thing you want in a program is to allow artificial barriers to impede the energy. This can mean taking over projects and initiatives, and people, that were not part of the program and were never expecting to be part of the program, but which are advantageous to adopt. This has even got a name, it's called 'brigading up.' (Figure 5.8[4])

Finally, there is one more form of boundary management involved in programs, and that is using boundaries to defend and nurture fragile initiatives within the program itself. Nascent ideas, often need time and

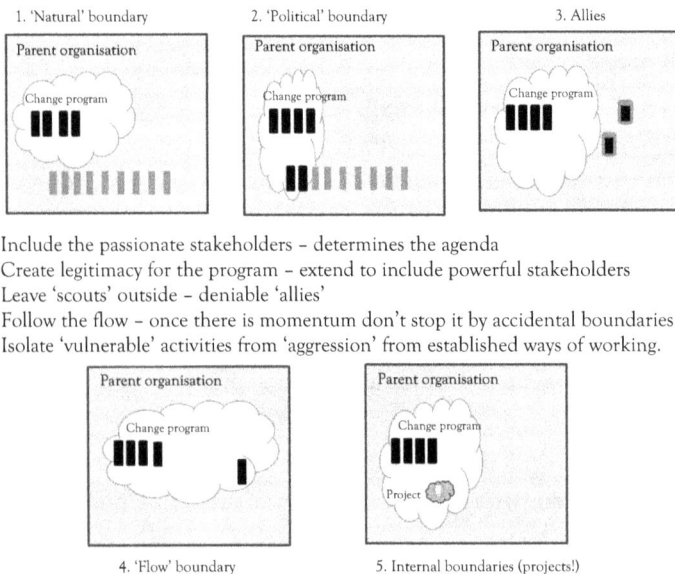

1. Include the passionate stakeholders – determines the agenda
2. Create legitimacy for the program – extend to include powerful stakeholders
3. Leave 'scouts' outside – deniable 'allies'
4. Follow the flow – once there is momentum don't stop it by accidental boundaries
5. Isolate 'vulnerable' activities from 'aggression' from established ways of working.

Figure 5.8 Boundary management situations

space to become established, and programs can do that when it is in their interests to do so. Programs are natural spaces to bring on innovative approaches in a protected and safe environment—giving the project sufficient time, attention and protection to allow ideas to be explored outside the harsh gaze of standard project governance processes (Figure 5.8[5]).

Program Management: Challenge 4: Balancing the Demands of Design, Delivery and Change

Challenge 4, 'Balancing the demands of design, delivery, and change' is genuinely difficult and is one of the reasons why many successful programs turn out to be run by management *teams* that explicitly reflect these three aspects of the program.

Figure 5.9 graphically illustrates the governance roles. The program directorate—the set of senior managers acting as role-based stakeholders (Worsley 2016)—who have oversight of the program are led by a senior responsible officer (SRO). The SRO connects the program management to the power bases in the organization, so things can get done.

Project delivery via the tranches demands the skills of a portfolio manager. Projects are managed by their project managers; the tranche is managed by the Delivery Manager.

The Design Authority manages the program structure and resultant interactions, as well as the management of the infrastructure and cost-risks

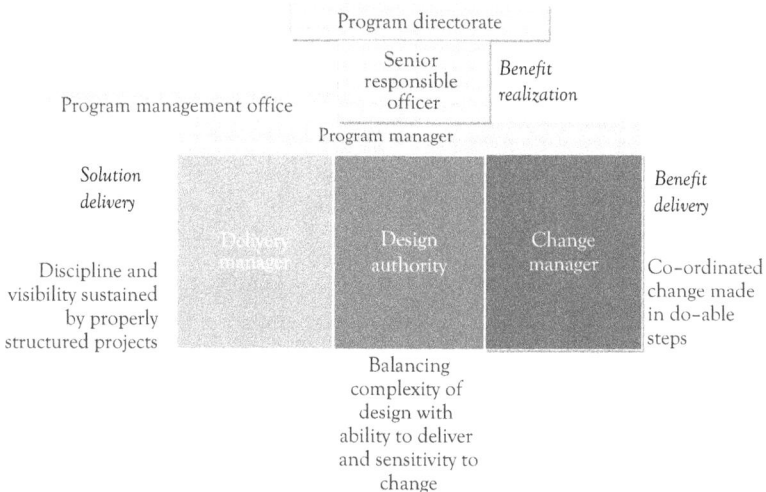

Figure 5.9 Program management roles

associated with the evolving solution. The Design Authority is not the designer of the solutions. The role is more like a business architect who integrates the various design threads into a coherent 'tapestry.'

Change is managed through a Business Change Manager role. This role is responsible for managing the benefit-risks, reducing, or eliminating the threats to achieving the beneficial outcomes.

It should be noted that these are roles, not jobs. The problem to be addressed is making sure that each of the three aspects of the program has a voice. There is no implication that there should be three people involved. It could be one very capable person or many. In one national bank, they ran a mega-program that had 18 people in the program management team: one Program Manager, three individuals acting as the Design Authority, five Delivery Managers, and nine Business Change Managers.

Program managers, like all of us, have preferences: some like analysis, some are action people wanting to get things done, for others it's innovation. Our decisions are biased by our preferences in subtle, unnoticed ways. So, programs benefit from planning that explicitly addresses the tension between design, delivery, and change, so a multi-person program team in some circumstances is valuable.

Program Management: Challenge 5: On-Boarding Change Teams

Challenge 5, 'On-boarding the change team,' is a special case of stakeholder engagement. At one level, these individuals are members of the program and subject to team management, but at another, they are agenda-based stakeholders.

Given that a program manager is judged on whether the vision has been achieved; on ensuring the outcomes are delivered, not the outputs of the projects, it's all about engagement, collaboration, and integrating project and operational effort. That is exactly where the change team, a mixture of change leaders, change agents, and change managers, comes in. It is easy to assume their agendas are aligned with the program, or perhaps irrelevant, and that would be a mistake. Just ask a few failed programs.

Change leader: The principle cause and motivator of change.

These are change sponsors and have governance accountability for ensuring that the appropriate financial and other resources are committed, issues are resolved, and the change succeeds. They need the authority, seniority, power, enthusiasm, and time to lead/carry through/oversee the changes. They agree the change strategy and approach, but do not usually get involved with the day-to-day management of the change. They monitor progress and visibly show their support of the process of change set in motion by change agents. They act as a promoter of the change process at the grass roots, keep the issues alive, help work out the implications and consequences and proposals for change at the organizational level. They must accept the ultimate responsibility for the successful change implementation.

Change manager is both a recognized job as well as a role.

Change managers have techniques, tools, and expertise to lead organizational change and personal change. They have responsibility for the detailed planning, monitoring, and control of the implementation of change actions across the organization and should be involved in designing the change process. This includes the communication strategy and contingency plans. They take responsibility and manage the change progress on a day-to-day basis. They typically facilitate key events to build commitment, liaise up, down and across the organizational structure and report progress to the change leader.

Change agents are individuals, who act as a catalyst and assume the responsibility for managing local, typically personal, change activities. They need to possess enough knowledge and power to guide and facilitate change efforts. Part of the change agent role is to be the trouble-shooter and apply transformational leadership to communicate the vision, act consistently to bring the vision into reality, and to build commitment in others to that vision. They are the genuine implementers of change—it is they who really make the difference, especially when it comes to implementing at a local level. Change agents have the influence and authority to translate the change into workplace realities as they have a good understanding of the business operations.

Their characteristic traits are:

- *Purpose*: They are aware of the need to change and share the vision of the future with the change sponsor.
- *Capability to act*: They are politically aware, possess interpersonal skills, and have at least structural or action leadership abilities.
- *Sells success*: They use techniques to promote the communication of success and focus on spreading new practices.
- *Strategically connected*: They are sources of power and influence.
- *Opportunistic*: They look for and use external and internal levers for change and are eclectic in their choice of resources. They strongly encourage innovation.

We have discussed the different roles that *program management* has to adopt. Figure 5.10 graphically illustrates how these roles interrelate. Notice, in particular, the change managers' remit and their closer association with the line managers and operatives than with the projects. Being more embedded in the current operations makes them more effective in their role, but it can also make their alignment to the program's vision more problematic as there is a danger of them getting involved with the local politics, a situation sometimes described as 'going native.'

Program Management: Challenge 6: Delivering Projects in a Program

The final challenge, Challenge 6, 'Delivering projects in a program— managing a tranche,' is really the same set of challenges any portfolio manager faces, with the added problem of the portfolio being embedded in a program.

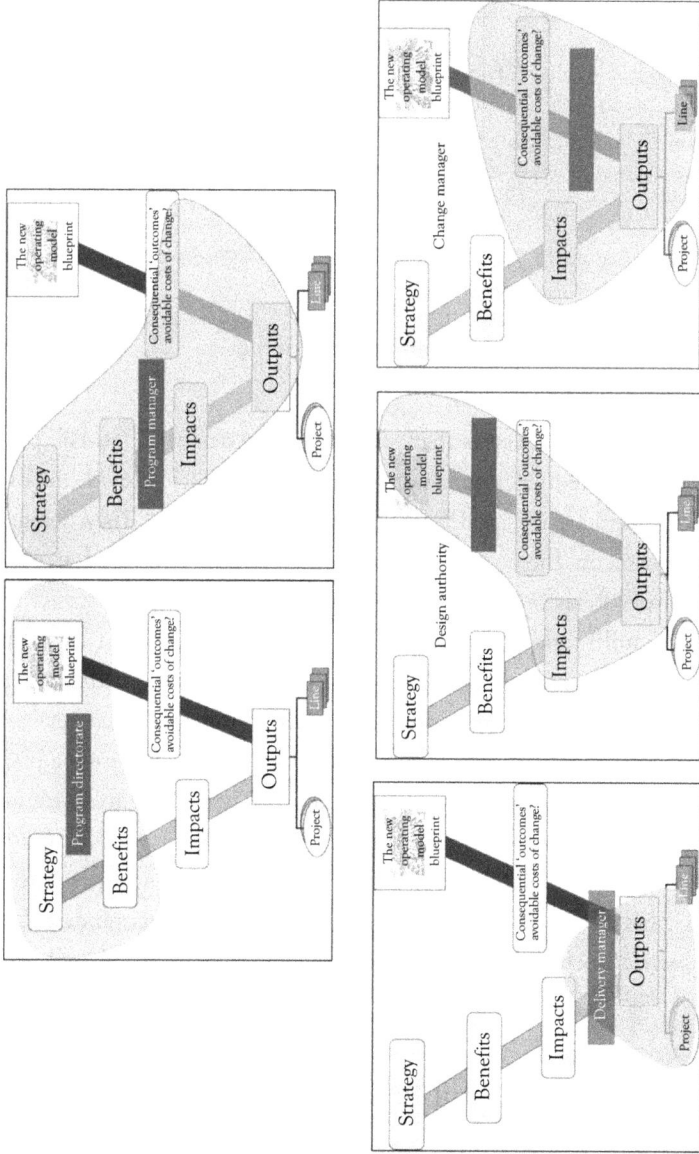

Figure 5.10 The remit of the program management roles

Impact on throughput

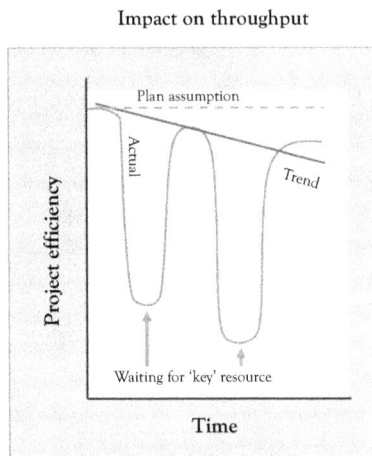

Figure 5.11 Impact of inappropriate resourcing

One of the special issues that raises is how to deal with 'no-fail' projects—we call them 'keystone' projects—because they provide pivotal capabilities and are essential to the delivery of the vision. They demand special treatment. The need for resource optimization is much clearer and has a sharper focus in program tranches. We have already discussed the impact of multi-tasking a resource across several projects and its significant negative impact on productivity. This consequence is difficult to accept on a keystone project, as is the impact on delivery when keystone projects are made to wait for resources. Figure 5.11 shows how the planning assumption about productivity is affected when resources are not immediately available when scheduled.

Other projects' needs are made subservient to delivering any keystone project. This is how to interpret the actions of the beach master described in the portfolio chapter when he protected the third of the three linked trucks.

A Successful Program Restructure

Let's look at a program that was set up to deal with the aftermath of the failure of a strategic project to deliver change in a private healthcare group. The business had seen its patient base decline while its cost base had risen steeply. There was an urgent need to reconfigure the medical resources and locations that it was using to deliver its services and to respond to the changing market dynamics. Clearly, an information-intensive solution was needed. IT offered a solution. It defined a strategic project in which it would establish a number of large-scale data centers, powerful analytics, and provide up-to-the-minute information as to the utilization of the medical resources.

The architecture of the solution, and the project plan to deliver it, stretched across several walls and was brightly colored to illustrate the different strands and threads of activity. After three years, and with no delivery of any value to the increasingly frustrated senior management, a demand for something to happen became irresistible. And many Heads of IT had been taken!

The new IT director decided that a programmatic approach was necessary. She identified that the value of the initiative was in the answering of the 20 most important questions that the Board had. So she deconstructed the problem and declared to the Board that she would be in a position to answer the first and most important question within four months. In each of the following tranches, she would be able to furnish the answers to three or four more.

The IT project managers, the data architects, the analyst-programmers, all cautioned her against this approach, saying that they would be unable to provide the information she required. When challenged, it became clear that in their view: "You can't have anything, until you have everything."

She helped to restructure their thinking, as well as the projects, and got them to focus on delivering exactly the information necessary to answer the two most important questions the Board had about medical resource utilization and location. She accepted that there would be a need for rework. As work progressed, information and data structures would become more complicated. As she pointed out to them: "Nobody asked you to solve the problem in the most efficient way. What are wanted are answers that address the Board's concerns now!"

She and the program delivered at just a bit better than the rate that she had set out. The Board now felt that it was back in control, that it was making decisions based upon real evidence. Within nine months they were asking IT if they required more money and more resources, rather than asking IT to cut budgets and demanding that they actually deliver something.

This approach: look to see where the value lies and deliver to that value, can be difficult for experienced IT project managers to accept. "How can deliberately planning to recode and reorganize data be sensible?" they say. But sometimes it just is!

Reflections

Many organizations have put programs into the 'too hard to do' box, partly because they try to use project-based concepts to manage them—which is definitely too hard. It is true that program governance costs are considerably higher than for a project. Programs demand business leadership and commitment far beyond that expected of the stakeholders in projects. Where project overheads are commonly between four and 12 percent, programs can be as high as 20 percent, so it is unwise to create programs unnecessarily.

In this chapter, we have discussed how programs are set up, structured and planned as well as the six challenges faced in planning a program:

- Getting the structure of a program right
- Translating a vision into everyday physical actions
- From management targets to stakeholder commitment
- Balancing the demands of design, delivery, and change
- On-boarding change teams
- Delivering projects in a program—managing a tranche

Consider these questions:

1. Under what circumstances would you recommend to your organization that it establishes a set of projects as a program rather than as a portfolio?
2. Do you have project boards or steering groups associated with projects running in your programs? How, if at all, does their role differ from that when looking after an independent project?

3. Managing scope is a central concern for project managers, while for program managers their focus is on issue management. How are issues tracked and communicated on your own programs?

4. In your own organization, how do programs involve line managers in the delivery of the program's vision? Are the line-based activities which fall within the boundary of the program, monitored? How?

5. How do you and your organization distinguish between project portfolios and programs?

CHAPTER 6

Developing Planning Expertise

What Skills and Competencies Matter?

In our research on what makes project managers successful (Worsley 2009; Wentworth 1998), we found that high performing project managers spent comparatively more time planning than less capable ones. So, we were disappointed to see in a recent review of project governance practices in five large project organizations, that in 25 percent of projects there was little evidence of planning having taken place.

Project managers often claim they are pressured to cut the planning and 'get on with the job.' Why they cave into this is less clear—many professions have clients who are unaware of the intricacies of what the job entails but when demands are made to make shortcuts to what they know to be fundamental procedures, do not readily accede. It is a rare surgeon who fails to 'scrub up' no matter how urgent the operation is!

Today, if you ask a project manager what the most important skill is that they require for their job, they are likely to refer to areas such as stakeholder management, communications, leadership, or other behavioral competencies. Is this because it is assumed that planning is important and does not need to be mentioned or is it that project managers believe that with the right leadership style, communications and engagement they don't need planning? Do approaches such as Agile, which expound people over process—promote this view of the obsolescence of planning?

To address the last question first, absolutely not! In his excellent book on Agile planning, Mike Cohn (2005) argues that while plans may be out-of-date by the time we commit them to paper, the *process* of planning is essential.

Estimating and planning are critical to the success of any software development project of any size or consequence. Plans guide our investment decisions…Plans help us know who needs to be available to work on a project during a given period. Plans help us know if a project is on track to deliver the functionality that users need and expect. Without plans, we open our projects to any number of problems.

What about leadership? Research on project management competence does highlight this as an essential component of project management but what is actually meant by this term is often unclear (Nijhuis et al. 2018). It has been variously defined as the ability to engage with others; to comprehend the project context; to display strategic vision; critical thinking; and emotional resilience (see Brière et al. 2015; Turner and Müller 2006). We could perhaps be forgiven for thinking that ultimately leadership turns out to be a framework term referring to a combination of behavioral (personal and inter-personal) competencies, which need to be more explicitly understood.

Behavioral competencies are undoubtedly important and have been neglected, particularly by the project management professional bodies. For example, it was not until Version 5.0 of the PMBOK (2013) that the PMI even included stakeholder management as a primary process. The competency models for the leading professional groups now include behavioral competencies, and links between them and overall project performance have been made. For example, Gruden and Stare (2018) found that more than one-third of the behavioral competencies they examined had a direct bearing on how well project managers performed. Their results suggest that 'assertiveness' is correlated with successful achievement. They also concluded competencies vary with the type of project.

In our research on the characteristics of successful project managers, which is discussed later in the chapter, it was found that good project managers have distinctive personality traits and behaviors. The main ones are:

- *Integrity* in project managers is observed as reporting situations truthfully; doing what they say they will; accepting the hard as well as the easy aspects of responsibility; communicating frankly with everyone whatever their level in the organization. This demands organizational bravery—'telling it as it is,' even if the news isn't welcome.

- *A strong achievement orientation.* This comes across as a need to complete and a drive to 'win.'
- *A focus on satisfying clients* and making strenuous efforts to communicate issues to senior management as they arise.
- *A design mindset and approach to planning.* A natural ability to solve complex multi-dimension problems using planning techniques. Planning is not an analysis problem; it is, more importantly, about structuring tasks, resources, risks, and schedules in ways that can be brought to a successful conclusion.

Successful project managers show these behaviors and especially, these personality traits from early in their careers, but they show them more emphatically as they develop. The characteristics of good project managers appear to converge as they gain experience. Although it is possible for people without these personality traits to become good project managers, it requires a modification of behaviors and attitudes. This is a far more difficult process than developing knowledge and skills and leads to the question: Are great project managers born or made?

Stop Looking for a Superhero Project Manager

In one of those memories passed down via family members, apparently, when Louise was a nine-year-old girl, she was asked what she wanted to be when she grew up. She responded by saying, "I want to be an expert," but wasn't sure in what! Whatever she meant then, today an expert is not someone who is characterized by their extensive personal repository of knowledge and judgment; there is too much information, too many insights, all of which is increasing exponentially, for that. Nowadays it's more to do with who is in your network, and which networks you work within that count. Stephenson (n.d.) captures the sense of it perfectly in her phrase, "I store my knowledge in my friends."

Much research over the last 20 years has attempted to identify the characteristics of successful project *managers*. More recently, however, this has been questioned and replaced with a more interesting debate. What makes for successful project *management*? The argument goes that even the 'best' project manager acting alone without support from the organization and without appropriate collaboration with peers and other stakeholders is unlikely to be successful. In our own research on the characteristics of high performing project managers, we found that they were much more likely to have extended personal and professional relationships within and outside their organizations. It wasn't just that they had more expertise to draw upon, but also that when they needed to interact with stakeholders, to further the goals of their projects, they were more likely to have pre-existing relationships to draw upon. They built up and valued 'social capital' in ways that less experienced project managers were unlikely to do.

Project *management* as a concept is important because first, it acknowledges that management is not the domain of the project manager alone but a bringing together of leadership, coordination, and drive from several different sources. Leadership and direction from sponsors and business owners must overlap and integrate with the leadership and coordination driven by the project manager. In complex projects and programs, there may be several roles involved in this 'management' process.

Project management also captures the idea that management goes beyond the roles, capabilities, and skills of individuals. It includes organizational, individual, and group competencies, which contribute to overall project capability within a project-based organization:

- *Individual capability*: The critical competencies that contribute to the success of individuals roles within a project (for example, the project manager, the sponsor, and so on).
- *Organizational capability*: The ability of the organization to develop and support processes, procedures and cultural acceptance of project management. The rising popularity of project offices is an attempt to address the projectization of organizations—the development of the so-called project-based-organization.
- *Collective capability*: The ability to create and exploit cooperative approaches to the achievement of project goals.

The idea is to combine competencies in order to produce outcomes that could not have been achieved by any one of them deployed in isolation. There appear to be parallels here with approaches taken within the Agile framework, which emphasizes the importance of collaborative structures, allowing developers and the business to work together in delivering the project goals.

There Is Not One Way of Being a Great Project Manager

It was back in 1989 when we asked the question, "Why is there so much variability in the performance of projects?" This was five years before the first CHAOS report by the Standish Group (1995) reported success rates of just 16 percent and failure rates of more than 30 percent. We didn't have those numbers, but we did know a project was not one of those things you could rely on to work.

We worked with CSC—the US computer company—to find an answer. In 1989, project methods were 'big.' There were many competing options and a lot of hype. We quickly discovered that though not having a method was a fairly sure path to project trouble, having one was no panacea. Performance could not be predicted by how well the method was used, and it certainly didn't matter which one was used—a dead end.

An alternative hypothesis was that it wasn't the method, it was the manager. All projects had a project manager; perhaps it was their influence that ultimately mattered. Was this a case of people over process? A thesis taken up many years later by the software product developers in their Agile Manifesto.

After reviewing and analyzing the characteristics of 263 project managers who had all successfully completed three or more projects one after the other we had an interesting problem. Statisticians told us that there were four clusters of competences (Figure 6.1). This was a significant result, but it was down to us to sort out what that might mean. The clusters simply indicated that high-performing project managers exhibited characteristic 'behaviors,' which was what we were looking for, but having four was a bit embarrassing. How can there be four ways of being good?

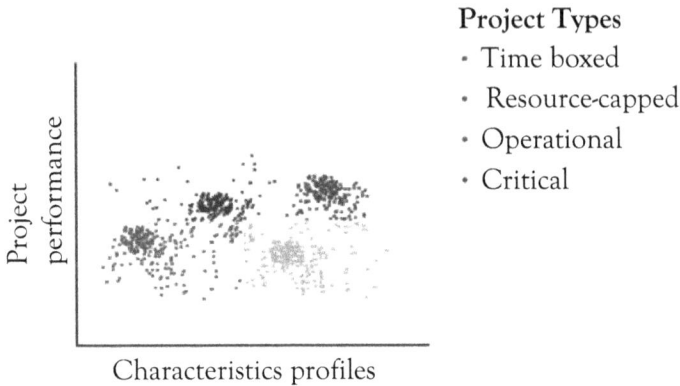

Project Types
- Time boxed
- Resource-capped
- Operational
- Critical

Figure 6.1 The four clusters

Identifying the *High-Performing Group (HPG)*. There is no single definition of what it means to be a successful project manager. For our
research we identified it as somebody who had run three successful
projects in a row, as agreed by the major stakeholders of the project;
the project manager, the manager of the project manager, the client,
and the team.

It turns out that this is quite a harsh judgment criterion. Of the
1500 project managers in our sample, only 263 met this condition.
These project managers were then assessed using a wide variety of
evaluation instruments. We called them the high-performance group
or HPG.

Some time and more money were spent, and we had the beginning
of an answer. Now, after more than 20 years and over 37,000 assessments
later, we are reasonably confident that the analysis reflects a genuine reality. There are different clusters of behaviors because there are different
categories of projects that are characterized by different sets of risk
judgments in the planning and execution of the project. The results are
shown in Figure 6.1.

The first of these types of projects we called 'end-date driven' projects.
These are the projects where missing the end-date would signal total failure of the project, and the planning and execution are based on ensuring
that does not happen. It involves making judgments and taking risks that
make attaining the end-date as likely as possible.

The second group we called 'resource-constrained' projects. In these projects, the problem fundamentally revolves around the fact that the resources available to solve the project problem are not shaped by the demands of the project. They are fixed and cannot be changed. The judgments and risk that now need to be taken are different from those of the end-date driven projects.

The third cluster was best characterized by the type of project management decisions taken by managers faced with running 'operational' projects. These include product-maintenance and similar projects, sometimes called enhancement projects in organizations that are faced with maintaining their core systems and capabilities by incremental improvements. The risks and judgments revolve around keeping the business running, rather than changing it.

The last distinct cluster was finally identified as those projects that were in some way 'mission-critical.' These were 'no-fail' projects, either because there were safety-critical aspects: nuclear, health, space, or because they really were business critical, with failure not being an option.

So, it turns out that the nature of the project changes the approach and style of management that the project manager needs to adopt. We even had a chance to test this in a case study-driven assessment center. Project managers were given a project that was clearly time constrained. They constructed their plans and then then we changed the scenario. As the project progressed, we introduced factors that meant the project was resource constrained. What we found was that the HPG managers would recognize the change and adapt their approach appropriately. The weaker, less experienced project managers did not.

It appears that project managers have a natural preference for one approach to project management over the others—and this varies from project manager to project manager. When there is a good match between the project type and project manager, then things are easier. If the match is poor—problems! Given this, naturally, the next question is: Is there such a thing as a professional project manager? Can you develop project managers to manage appropriately irrespective of the type of project they find themselves in? The short answer, from a lot of hard work, is that you can. Not everyone, and sometimes not easily, because it is about attitudes as well as knowledge and skill, but it can be done—but it goes a long way beyond knowledge of a method.

Why Judgment Matters in Project Management

We now believe there are at least seven different project types, with seven distinct sets of risk judgments that affect the planning approach chosen.

- Schedule-driven planning
- Resource-driven planning
- Budget-constrained planning
- Operational—When it has to fit into operational imperatives
- Mission critical—When it really does have to work
- Stakeholder-led—When stakeholder engagement is critical
- Innovation—When it has to be different

We discuss each of these in *Adaptive Project Planning* (Worsley and Worsley 2019).

For each of these seven types, the planning approach varies and the plans created are not interchangeable. If the conditions of success for a project changes, for example, it moves from being operational to budget-constrained, the project needs to be re-planned. And the reality is that some projects do change their nature in-flight. A project may initially be driven by a hard deadline, but then issues arise that can only be resolved by acquiring scarce resources and the characteristics of the project change fundamentally, and a re-plan is fundamental.

What seems to be the distinguishing quality of the HPG project managers is that they are much more capable at both recognizing these changes and at adjusting their approaches to meet the new challenges. How the HPG develop this ability is a crucial question for project managers and those involved in their personal and professional development. Is it a function of behavioral competencies such as flexibility and adaptability or more complex factors such as Emotional Intelligence—relationship to self-awareness, and awareness of our environment? Is it something that comes about as a result of experience and exposure to many different types of projects? We certainly found that experience—the variety and breadth of experiences—was the highest correlate with overall project management performance. The answer probably lies in a combination of all of these factors, summed up in a capability we refer to as 'judgment.'

Developing High Performing Project Managers

If you ask a project manager how they got into project management, you are likely to find that at some point in their career they 'fell into the role.' They were involved in some area, engineering, construction, IT, and so on and somebody said—"Hey, you are good at this. Could you run this project for us?" In some cases, they were offered support and training, but more often than not they were just thrown in at the deep end and had to learn on-the-job. Until recently it was reasonably rare for project managers to have pursued project management as a conscious career decision. (Consider yourself: How did you get into managing projects, and why have you stayed?)

CITI commissioned research on project manager performance, and the role subject matter expertise had on how well the project turned out. It was carried out at the University of Limerick and was based on data CITI had collected. It would seem there is a choice to be made as to whether to continue as an SME and acquire project management skills, or become a professional project manager. (The results of this research are discussed more fully, later in this chapter.)

In developing from novices (new-to-projects) through to experienced professionals (running complex projects), project managers may be described as progressing through three distinct stages (Figure 6.2).

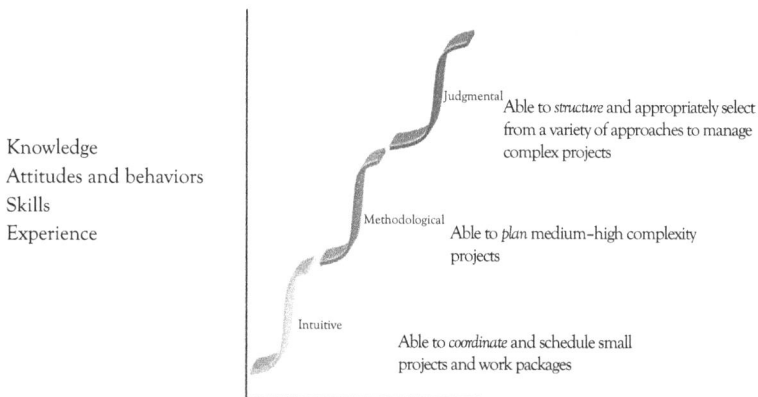

Knowledge
Attitudes and behaviors
Skills
Experience

Judgmental — Able to *structure* and appropriately select from a variety of approaches to manage complex projects

Methodological — Able to *plan* medium–high complexity projects

Intuitive — Able to *coordinate* and schedule small projects and work packages

Figure 6.2 The IMJ model: differing PM capabilities

The *intuitive* stage is typified by those experiences you may have had when you first started in projects. They chose you, because you seemed to have good organizing skills, got things done, could be relied upon. You had a recognizable aptitude for project coordination. Many project offices promote career paths for junior administrative roles into project management, but you may have noticed that not all the administrators make it. Some of them are successful in project support roles but seem to lack the style, approach, and empathy for coordination, which is the basis for a potential project manager. Not everybody makes it through the intuitive stage. They may reside in this area, running small projects and work packages or may combine project skills with other roles. A typical combination in IT, for example, is a business analyst/project manager.

The intuitive stage is where junior project managers (JPM) build their confidence, and they begin to understand what works and what doesn't. With their intuitive understanding and natural coordination skills, managers will perform well initially but are likely to struggle or even fail, as projects get larger and more complex. When projects that are more complex are given to them, JPMs may feel 'stressed,' unable to cope. They often find the workload is higher than they can manage—they are being asked to operate at a level, which is beyond their current experience and knowledge of projects.

To deal with the greater variety of challenges and new sources of complexity, managers must draw upon more than innate capability. They need to have access to the received wisdom and understanding of the professional community. We call this the 'methodological' stage, not because it demands the use of specific methods, but because managers are now able to use a publicly repeatable process. Unlike the intuitive stage, they do not have to re-invent the process and approach—they are able to draw upon and consistently apply recognized practices.

Intuitive. At this level, the emphasis is on technical leadership with less attention paid to the procedural, planning and monitoring aspects of project management. They are most successful when the project manager can visualize the product, and there is little cross-functional working.

Methodological. Here the emphasis is on product analysis, control, and network planning with heavy dependence on method-based approaches. This is most successfully deployed when used on large but relatively non-complex 'build' projects.

Judgmental. The focus here is on the delivery of outcomes rather than outputs. It is characterized by a holistic approach to project management with the emphasis on meeting stakeholder concerns and linking the outputs from the project to specific outcomes or project benefits.

In the 1990s, UK government promoted training in the PRINCE2® method. Their aim was to accelerate the creation of high performing project managers: a well-intentioned idea, but one that lacked an understanding of how professional skills actually develop. One of the unintended consequences of this was that ill-informed employers were given the impression that having a PRINCE2® qualification was indicative of the quality of the project managers' skills and competencies. As is now widely accepted, attending a training course, passing the PRINCE2® exam, or any other exam-based accreditation, does not make you a safe or good project manager. Indeed our experience as accredited trainer-providers is that test-taking skills and general intelligence are higher correlates with pass rates than actual ability and performance to run projects.

So is knowledge acquisition important for project managers in their career development? An analysis of our data collected from profiling over 37,000 project managers shows that high performing project managers are very unlikely to display low knowledge levels (as evidenced by the results from knowledge and skill tests). This suggests that getting an understanding of terms and project processes does matter.

Figure 6.3 is an analysis of the knowledge levels (assessed through a knowledge test) across project managers rated from novice to high performer through an independent assessment process. As we can see here, most of the high performers, approx. 95%, achieved an average or high mark on the knowledge test. However, 40% of the novice project managers also achieved average or above. It is entirely possible for somebody to perform well on a knowledge test and not be a high performing project manager. Knowledge about project management (as described in the various project management Bodies of Knowledge) and an appreciation of repeatable processes, methods such as PRINCE2® and other similar

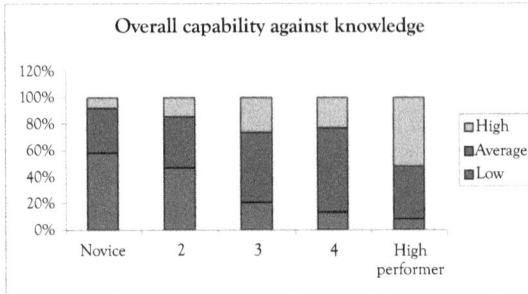

Figure 6.3 Knowledge and overall capability (Worsley 2009)

frameworks are undoubtedly important to the development of project capability. They are just not sufficient.

At the intuitive level, JPMs may work mostly on similar types of projects. The methodological level of development is characterized by the build-up of project knowledge and skills and the exposure and learning from experiences in a much larger variety of projects. At the methodological levels, for real progression to occur, the range of experiences and responsibilities taken must expand. In our HPG (those working at the judgmental level) we found that the average number of years' experience in project management was 10 years with a minimum of eight years. It was also clear that 10 years of the same experiences is not the same as 10 years working on a variety of projects. During the methodological stage, project managers grow their breadth of experience, and this forms the basis upon which judgment is developed.

So, an understanding of process and procedures is a necessary part of the project managers' development. As they get involved with larger projects and as their projects get more complex, they find that methods and procedures alone are not enough. Now the critical skill is the ability to mix and match approaches. To have the common sense to use tried and tested practices whenever appropriate, but to have the confidence to step off that path and structure new ways of working when these approaches are just not right. This is what we call the judgmental stage.

Breaking Through Glass Ceilings

You may have noticed that the IMJ development curves are represented by S-curves suggesting that there is a 'barrier' between the levels. These

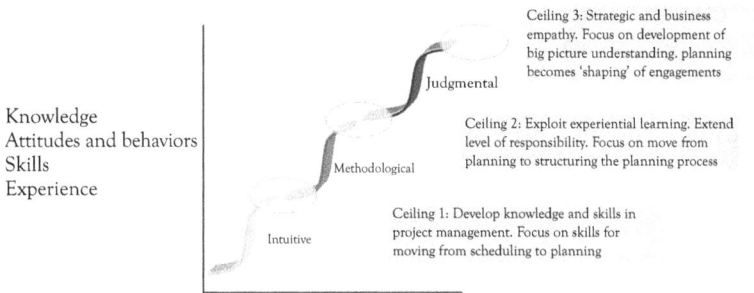

Ceiling 3: Strategic and business empathy. Focus on development of big picture understanding. planning becomes 'shaping' of engagements

Judgmental

Ceiling 2: Exploit experiential learning. Extend level of responsibility. Focus on move from planning to structuring the planning process

Methodological

Ceiling 1: Develop knowledge and skills in project management. Focus on skills for moving from scheduling to planning

Intuitive

Knowledge
Attitudes and behaviors
Skills
Experience

Figure 6.4 The glass ceilings

glass ceilings are significant in that they represent a change in the attitudes, skills, and behaviors needed to progress and safely manage more substantial and more complex projects (see Figure 6.4).

Ceiling 1: *intuitive to methodological* At some point, the project manager will need training to progress to the methodological level. This may take the form of accredited training such as PMP, IAPM qualifications, or indeed PRINCE2®. It may also involve undergraduate and postgraduate programs that include project management. An interesting question is whether this training should take place before or after the project manager has gained some experience. Our view is that it is better to expose new project managers to project challenges before they go on courses such as PRINCE2® as without context the lessons learned from the training are quickly lost.

During the intuitive stage, JPMs are building experiences of working on small projects or work packages. They may report to a more senior project manager providing planning and administrative support. The skill that must be learned to progress into the methodological stage—to be safe to manage more complex projects—is planning. And here we most definitely mean planning—not scheduling. While JPMs may be given the task of recording and modeling activities (using packages such as MS Project), this is not sufficient to provide them with an appreciation of how to scope a project and how to develop the project baselines against which the project will be monitored and managed.

In summary, the most important things we can do for our JPMs is to structure training episodes into their work experience and to support them in practicing the development of plans—in particular working with users and other technical experts to develop the scope of the project.

Ceiling 2: methodological to judgmental Project managers are likely to operate at the methodological stage for at least three to four years and indeed may never develop or be required to reach the judgmental level. The reason for this is twofold. Firstly, organizations don't need lots of high performing project managers, and therefore the opportunities to work on the most complex projects are often limited. There are problems also associated with having high performing project managers working on low complexity projects. Our findings suggest that the HPG managers when given relatively simple projects may actually create unnecessary complexity. As emphasized by research such as (Turner and Müller 2006)—the trick seems to be to attempt to match the skills of the project manager to the complexity of the project.

Apart from the lack of opportunity, the other element of the glass ceiling would appear to be the change in behaviors and attitudes necessary to run projects that are more complex. At this level, it's about having experience, conviction of actions, and perhaps even bravery. These project managers are working on high profile projects and must be able to face the challenges of operating under the very public scrutiny of many senior business stakeholders. Their approaches must be backed by the experience and professional understanding which allows them to make judgments about how best to structure the project for successful delivery. These project managers understand that the structure of the project must be adapted to the characteristics of the project.

In our profiling case studies, we provide situations for senior project managers where the characteristics of a project are changed, and they then re-evaluate their approaches. An example of this would be to alter the resourcing of a project, say moving from a co-located team to virtual teams delivering tightly integrated products. Less experienced project managers will recognize that this will change the nature of the communications process. More experienced projects managers will realize that this demands a more fundamental change—a change in the way that they choose to structure the work packages within the project.

Perhaps the most significant change in behaviors from methodological to judgmental is in the level of responsibility that the project manager is allowed and prepared to take on board. You don't successfully run complex projects without the ability to evaluate the risks and returns of a particular approach. Ultimately, the HPG managers in our research did not wait for the change in the project context and then react to it—they were able to anticipate the challenges (they had seen them before), and they proactively reframed the structure and planning process.

Ceiling 3: beyond judgmental What is the nature of the 'next step' for highly capable project managers at the judgmental level? It seems natural to consider program management, but our assessment of many projects and programs, and many project managers and program managers, suggest that whatever else it is, it's not natural. Over half of the 154 successful program managers we have profiled did not have project management backgrounds. And a disproportionate number of programs we were engaged to assist because they were failing were being led by very experienced project managers.

One of the characteristics in these cases was that there was a noticeable lack of tolerance for ambiguity in the planning and structuring of the program, and in the engagement with the stakeholders. In projects, this need to drive out uncertainty, striving for clarity of scope, is an admirable thing, and almost part of the job description. This is decidedly not the situation in a program, where maintaining ambiguity and flexible boundaries for as long as possible is often an essential aspect of the program managers' role.

So how should organizations promote the development of high performing project managers? In the late 1990s, BAE Systems launched a development program targeting its top 50 project managers. It was an innovative approach, which provided personal development and support structures to ensure that these managers would be successful on some of the biggest, most complex, and most challenging of programs. We were already involved in looking at what made project managers successful in BAE, and we got to interview and job shadow the managers running their big programs, such as the Eurofighter. These high performing managers had all been involved in project and program management for at least 20 years. An interesting and possibly crucial commonality in their career progression was that every single one of them had, at some point, been taken under the wing of a senior manager in the organization. Every single one of them cited the importance of having a mentor in the organization in their career development. Is it from this experience that they learned the value of tolerating uncertainty and making progress in the face of ambiguous and complex agendas?

Project Planning and Organizational Competences

When I ask them for plans they say they don't have the information. Don't they realize that planning means going and getting the information? What's the point of planning if you already know everything? Walking the plan, finding what will work, how can they not think this is part of their job?

—Program Manager

I'm spending all of my time trying to manage the resources for the portfolio!. We desperately need planning information from the projects, but some of the project managers just don't seem to know how to produce even the simplest plans.

—Portfolio Manager

This year we have let go four project managers even though we are desperately short of them. On paper, they looked good; they had all the right accreditations and experience. However, when it came down to it, they seemed unable to create and share plans on their projects. There was always some excuse as to why it wasn't worth doing the plan now.

—Project Office Manager

The frustration expressed by these program, portfolio, and project office managers with the lack of project planning skills in their project managers is not unusual. Charged with significant amounts of a company's investment money these managers are aware of the need to manage downside risks. They also know that if project managers are to earn and retain the trust needed to act as the single point of accountability that underpins the powerbase of project managers, being seen to be in control is fundamental. That means having a plan.

As we have seen in the journey toward judgmental project management discussed earlier, improving planning practices is not about sending people on training courses. It is about exposing individuals to challenging situations with an appropriate level of support: coaching or mentoring. In 2018, the PMO Global Alliance organization ran a competition to find the best project offices in the world. Each one of the finalists—the top performing project offices—specifically identified in their presentations the need to create a culture of project excellence across their businesses. What should organizations be doing to develop a level of excellent project performance?

Value Professional Project Managers

We were working with a large financial institution that had completely restructured its middle management. The organizational structure chart now showed a Projects Group with 26 project managers in it. How were these selected, we asked. "Oh," came the reply, "these were the people left when all the others had been allocated to jobs." We think they meant to say 'proper' jobs but were too shy to say it aloud.

In a large and important bank, we were asked to review the causes of the failure of two of their large projects. In both projects, the named project manager was a very senior manager in the organization. When we asked why they had been appointed, we were told the projects were so important that they had to be managed by a board member—despite the fact these people had no project management experience, empathy, or training. The cause of the failures was not hard to find!

In our research into the roles of project managers in 2009, we surveyed over 3,600 people who were actively managing projects (Worsley 2009). Of these, 80 percent had project-related job titles—project manager, project leader, program manager, or similar. The other 20 percent of people running projects had over 200 job titles between them, and they certainly did not identify themselves as or with project managers. That's one in five projects.

Back in the year 2000, we had been interested to know whether projects were better run by subject matter experts (SMEs) such as engineers, IT, and marketers, or by specialist project managers. Research conducted on some of CITI's data at the University of Limerick (Leonard and Willis 2000) investigated the impact of domain specialism of project managers on project performance.

The results are illuminating, and they make clear why the debate is so difficult to settle. The findings show that when the success factors are related to the content of the project—when satisfying the requirements is at the top of the stakeholders' agenda—the weight of evidence supports the proposition that the project is better run by an SME who has reasonably good project management understanding. When, however, the projects have complex structures with the constraints not being related to the content, such as time, cost, or stakeholder concerns, then the projects were much more likely to be successful when run by specialist project managers rather than SMEs.

The discipline of project management is commonly undervalued by organizations. Many projects, especially complex projects, demand significant project management expertise and do not perform well without it.

Confusing Product Expertise and Project Management

Working with Rolls Royce in the 1990s, we were discussing project performance and the problems of finding good project managers. We had supposed that such a prestigious engineering company would be a honeypot for such people. The senior engineer explained, "The problem is that what attracts people to Rolls Royce is engineering—the people we get are engineers, first-class engineers. They love engineering, and they are very good at it." The unspoken words are that being a brilliant engineer does not necessarily make you a good or even an adequate project manager. Many industries (engineering, construction, and IT) struggle with this issue.

This problem is exacerbated by organizations that have career paths that require a transition into management, with project management seen as the normal route. A sad case of the Peter Principle: organizations recruit, and develop excellence in technical skills and then promote these same people into roles and jobs they cannot do.

Recently there has been a focus by Project Management Professional Bodies (PMI and APM) on how to create career paths within project management. Perhaps the real solution lies in ensuring that technical progression paths also exist so that technical experts are not forced into positions they may not be suitable for, and may not even wish to follow.

Single Point of Accountability Still Matters

So, we would like to leave you with a final thought, and it is a return to the idea about the need for a single point of accountability in the conduct of a project.

Projects are *a temporary organization set up to manage the inherent uncertainty caused when resources are assigned to undertake a unique and transient endeavor within a set of constraints*. As such, they have no natural power base and no legitimate authority. These have to be gifted to it through structures like project boards and a project sponsor. The need to get things done requires this power to flow in clear and obvious channels.

With the introduction of more specialist project roles, as well as new levels of governance (it is not unusual to find four or more layers of governance for a project), with portfolio committees, project boards, IT infrastructure committees, and business architecture groups all vying for a say in the running of a project, deciding who is responsible for what gets more and more confusing (Figure 6.5).

We have sat in meetings with project managers who are convinced that all the communications and benefits planning will be done by the change manager only to be told by the change manager that it certainly was not their job!

We have worked with sponsors who see the project office as their go-to place for discussing project issues—not something they expect the project manager to get involved with.

Roles such as project office manager has now become a specialist route with its own professional development path and separate qualifications. It is not unusual now that a project office head will have little or no experience in running projects.

In all of this, what we consider to be in the end the *raison d'etre* of project management is lost. Some person—or at most a small tightly knit group—is charged with, is trusted with, and ultimately is accountable for the execution of a set of tasks within a precisely defined set of constraints by a temporary organizational structure, and that is the project manager. Project managers just have to be good enough to realize this.

The business case? Not my job... the business does that.

Requirements? Not my job... the business analyst does that.

The communications plan? Not my job... the communications manager does that.

Business reporting? Not my job...the program manager does that.

Stakeholder engagement? Not my job... the change manager does that.

Status updates? Not my job...the project office does that.

Project documentation? Not my job... the project administrator does that.

Quality assurance? Not my job... the test manager does that.

Workshops lead? Not my job... the facilitator does that.

Risk plans? Not my job... the risk manager does that.

Team management? Not my job... the line manager does that.

Resource allocation? Not my job... the portfolio manager does that.

Procurement? Not my job... the procurement manager does that.

Leadership? Not my job ... the sponsor does that.

Figure 6.5 Requiem for the project manager

Reflections

Throughout this chapter, we have emphasized the importance of adapting your approach to planning and your management style. Making judgments based on experience and know-how—the models you know and use—is the critical differentiator of the high performing project manager. You may be in an environment where the projects face you with the same problems—over and over. OK, good! You now have an opportunity to hone your skills and develop a deeper understanding of these types of projects. But beware, just because every swan you have ever seen has been white doesn't mean the next one will be! The next project may be different.

The superhero project manager does not, or should not exist. (All right, we know you are one really!). Ultimately, however, it's about how you, your stakeholders, and your organization get to be more capable of delivering projects.

Consider for yourself and your organization:

1. At what level of the intuitive, methodological, judgmental continuum would you position yourself? Why?
2. Do you recognize the glass-ceilings described in this chapter? What, if anything do you need to do to overcome your glass ceiling?
3. How are you using your personal and professional networks to support you in your project management role? Could you do more?
4. Does your organization promote the culture of project management? How?
5. What additional support would you like to see your organization provide to develop your project management expertise?

References

Boehm, B.W. 1981. *Software Engineering Economics*, 197 vols. Englewood Cliffs, NJ: Prentice-hall.

Brière, S., D. Proulx, O.N. Flores, and M. Laporte. 2015. "Competencies of Project Managers in International NGOs: Perceptions of Practitioners." *International Journal of Project Management* 33, no. 1, pp. 116–25.

Change Diamond™ is a Registered Trademark of CITI Limited.

Cohn, M. 2005. *Agile Estimating and Planning*. Pearson Education.

Flyvbjerg, B., N. Bruzelius, and W. Rothengatter. 2003. *Megaprojects and Risk: An Anatomy of Ambition*. Cambridge University Press.

Goldratt, E.M., and J. Cox. 1984. *The Goal, Croton-on-Hudson*. New York, NY: North River Press Inc.

Gruden, N., and A. Stare. 2018. "The Influence of Behavioral Competencies on Project Performance." *Project Management Journal* 49, no. 3, pp. 98–109.

Leonard, D., and L. Willis. 2000. "Is Project Manager Capability Domain Specific?" Congress 2000 Proceedings, IPMA.

Nijhuis, S., R. Vrijhoef, and J. Kessels. 2018. "Tackling Project Management Competence Research." *Project Management Journal* 49, no. 3, pp. 62–81.

Parker, M.M., R.J. Benson, and H.E. Trainor. 1988. *Information Economics: Linking Business Performance to Information Technology*. Englewood Cliffs, NJ: Prentice-Hall.

PRINCE2® is a Registered Trademark of AXELOS.

Project Management Institute (PMI). 2013. *A Guide to the Project Management Body of Knowledge (PMBOK® Guide)*, 5th ed. Newtown Square, PA: Author.

Project Mission Model™ is a Registered Trademark of CITI Limited.

Shenhar, A.J., O. Levy, and D. Dvir. 1997. "Mapping the Dimensions of Project Success." *Project Management Journal* 28, no. 2, pp. 5–13.

Stephenson, K. n.d. "What Knowledge Tears Apart, Networks Make Whole." Internal Communication, no. 36. Retrieved December 10, 2004 from http://netform.com/html/icf.pdf

Turner, J.R. 1999. *Gower Handbook of Project Management*, 4th ed. Aldershot, UK: Gower Publishing.

Turner, J.R., and R. Müller. 2003. "On the Nature of the Project as a Temporary Organization." *International Journal of Project Management* 21, no. 1, pp. 1–8.

Turner, J.R., and R. Müller. 2006. *Choosing Appropriate Project Managers: Matching their Leadership Style to the Type of Project*. Project Management Institute.

Wentworth Research. 1998. *Project Management.* The IT Management Programme (The CITI Research Was Documented in the Wentworth Report and Can be Accessed Via the Website Links that Accompany this Book).

Wheelwright, S.C., and K.B. Clark. 1992. *Revolutionizing Product Development: Quantum Leaps in Speed, Efficiency, and Quality.* Simon and Schuster.

Worsley, L.M. 2009. "The Characteristics of Successful Project Managers: Insights from Across Sector Profiling of Project Managers." AIPM Conference, *Modernisation in Project Management.* Adelaide, Australia.

Worsley, L.M. 2010. "Remploy–A Case of Super-Sensitive, Stakeholder Management." *The Project Manager,* 6 (accessed September 2010).

Worsley, L.M. 2016. *Stakeholder-Led Project Management: Changing the Way We Manage Projects.* Business Expert Press.

Worsley, L.M., and C.J. Worsley. 2019. *Adaptive Project Planning.* Business Expert Press. http://pmknowledgecenter.com/dynamic_scheduling/risk/critical-chainbuffer-management-adding-buffers-project-schedule (accessed August 16, 2018).

About the Authors

Louise Worsley has been a project management consultant, lecturer, and coach for nearly 30 years. She is a visiting lecturer at the University of Cape Town on the MSc in Project Management.

Louise is a regular contributor to project management online forums, a judge in the Global Alliance PMO Awards, joint leader of the Success Stories Shared PMSA initiative to encourage the sharing of experiences and learning across the project manager community, and author of "Stakeholder-led Management: Changing the way we manage projects" (Worsley 2016).

Christopher Worsley has been the CEO of CITI Limited since 1991. CITI is a UK-based company dedicated to developing organizational and personal capabilities in project and program management within corporate organizations and government. He has been involved in the development project and program management as practiced in the UK for over 45 years, including the launch of PRINCE2® and a number of PM accreditations.

Christopher has worked on over 150 transformation programs—either as program manager, program architect or as a lead assessor on program assurance teams. He is a senior advisor on project and program performance to a number of large corporations in South Africa and the UK.

Index

OTHER TITLES IN OUR PORTFOLIO AND PROJECT MANAGEMENT COLLECTION

Timothy J. Kloppenborg, Editor

- *Project Portfolio Management: A Model for Improved Decision Making* by Clive N. Enoch
- *Project Management Essentials* by Kathryn Wells and Timothy J. Kloppenborg
- *The Agile Edge: Managing Projects Effectively Using Agile Scrum* by Brian Vanderjack
- *Project Teams: A Structured Development Approach* by Vittal S. Anantatmula
- *Attributes of Project-Friendly Enterprises* by Vittal S. Anantatmula and Parviz F. Rad
- *Stakeholder-led Project Management: Changing the Way We Manage Projects* by Louise M. Worsley
- *Innovative Business Projects: Breaking Complexities, Building Performance, Volume One: Fundamentals and Project Environment* by Rajagopal
- *Innovative Business Projects: Breaking Complexities, Building Performance, Volume Two: Financials, New Insights, and Project Sustainability* by Rajagopal
- *Why Projects Fail: Nine Laws for Success* by Tony Martyr
- *Project-Based Learning: How to Approach, Report, Present, and Learn from Course-Long Projects* by Harm-Jan Steenhuis and Lawrence Rowland

Announcing the Business Expert Press Digital Library

Concise e-books business students need for classroom and research

This book can also be purchased in an e-book collection by your library as

- a one-time purchase,
- that is owned forever,
- allows for simultaneous readers,
- has no restrictions on printing, and
- can be downloaded as PDFs from within the library community.

Our digital library collections are a great solution to beat the rising cost of textbooks. E-books can be loaded into their course management systems or onto students' e-book readers.
The **Business Expert Press** digital libraries are very affordable, with no obligation to buy in future years. For more information, please visit **www.businessexpertpress.com/librarians**. To set up a trial in the United States, please email **sales@businessexpertpress.com**.

www.ingramcontent.com/pod-product-compliance
Lightning Source LLC
Chambersburg PA
CBHW061324220326
41599CB00026B/5016